TELEGARBAGE

by
GREGG A. LEWIS

FOREWORD BY JIM JOHNSON

THOMAS NELSON INC., PUBLISHERS
Nashville • New York

Third printing

Library of Congress Cataloging in Publication Data

Lewis, Gregg A
  Telegarbage.

  Includes bibliographical references.
  1. Television broadcasting—United States—Moral and
religious aspects. I. Title.
PN1992.6.L48   348.55'4'0973   77-24093
ISBN 0-8407-5628-3

Contents

Foreword 11
1 Big Brother is Watching 17
2 Big Brother is Being Watched! 31
3 Mayhem in the PM: The Behavior Transfer 43
4 Sex in the Script 57
5 Telebucks: A View from the Bottom Line . 71
6 The Perils of Cause and Effect 85
7 Tele-addiction: "God Help the Children" . 97
8 The Control Room at Home 111
9 Fighting Back: Fencing in the Dump! 123
10 Creating Some Alternatives 135
11 A Final Word 149
   Appendix 153
   Footnotes 157

Acknowledgements

Special thanks and love go to my wife, Debi, for her contribution to my writing and my life. Her questions, insights, encouragement, support, and love kept me thinking and writing.

Thanks too should go to my mentor and friend, Jim Johnson, for his collaboration on this work. His teaching, his advice, and his journalistic example have prodded and inspired me.

Appreciation is also due my friends and professors, both at Wheaton and Asbury colleges. Their teachings sharpened and equipped me with a Christian perspective on communication and on life.

Grateful acknowledgement is also extended to the officials of the national Parent-Teacher Association. They generously cooperated in the research for this book by opening their files of testimonies given at their 1977 public hearings on TV and violence.

Gregg A. Lewis

This book is dedicated with deepest love, gratitude, and respect to my parents for their constant love, support, and Christian examples—the ingredients that enabled me to survive, grow, and mature to adulthood as part of the television generation.

TELEGARBAGE

Foreword

When George Orwell wrote his book *1984* thirty or so years ago, it was considered to be purely science fiction. The idea of a society controlled and dominated by "Big Brother"—a television set—was unthinkable, if not actually ludicrous.

But the horror of that fiction has now become a reality. For millions, "Big Brother" is already here in living rooms, family rooms, recreational rooms, even bedrooms, or wherever the electronic eye can be put for easy access. Every year millions of people become its willing captives, unaware that their minds are being programmed by a dazzling, bloody array of violence and sex unprecedented in electronic communication history.

In the last five years in particular there has been a dangerous shift in television programming from an attempt (feeble as it was) at keeping some kind of balance in terms of light and wholesome entertainment to a bald, blatant, bawdy format designed to titillate and tickle the new society's penchant for the sensational.

Parents who had shunned X-rated films in the

local theater for themselves and their children now get and seemingly tolerate the same kind of fare in their homes. Nude couples in bed, demonstrating sexual activity, coupled with vulgar lines in popular sit-coms, combined with scenes of rape and homosexual attacks, are visuals constantly pulverizing the brains of young and old alike.

Shootings, brutal ax killings, strangulations, eye gougings, castrations, and scalpings come pouring through the "family hour" so graphically that afterward children, even up to fourteen and fifteen years of age, find it too terrifying to sleep alone. Others, as is now proved, try to ape what they see, believing that a good karate chop, a "Saturday-night special," or a switchblade will get for them what it appears to have gotten the characters on the screen. One only has to sit in juvenile court on any Saturday morning to catch the grim, terrible tragedy of the young who have been duped by "Big Brother" to go out and do likewise.

This is not to say there is no good at all in television. Somehow, in the mayhem coming across "bloody and burlesque alley," as the family hour is now called, there are honest and genuine attempts to communicate values worth emulating and information and insights of immense significance to viewers. But one week of "Roots" or a few episodes of "Little House on the Prairie" or "The Waltons" do not adequately balance the heavy end of what is at best the prurient fare that covers at least 80 percent of TV programming.

To be fair, at least Public Television in America today is seeking to bring some kind of balance. But since it is forced to draw on public fund-raising to maintain itself, its contribution continues to remain peripheral to the big networks.

In the meantime, the public remains mute concerning "Big Brother," neither casting a vote for the few good things that come over the eye nor protesting the increasing majority of material that is hardly fit for human consumption. Each night families stay glued to the box, their eyes glazing with the full-color images of what they could hardly conjure up in their own fantasies, willing captives of a mind-binder that bends and shapes values and morals to its own predetermined design.

All of this is even more serious to the Christian family and the institutions charged with some sense of moral rightness. The fact that God's own people imbibe the same fare as their secular counterparts—without a whimper—is a serious contradiction to the Lord's commission to be "a light set on a hill." The fact that Christian families now own one or more TV sets and that far too many polled for this book are not seeking ways to bring order into their own households with regard to its use is nothing short of disturbing. "If the salt has become tasteless, . . . it is good for nothing any more" is the way the Lord put it concerning this kind of winking of the eye in terms of moral courage and spiritual character (Matt. 5:13).

The Christian value system is rooted in the principle of "righteousness," which is character and "rightness." If the Christian allows himself to be carried along by the tide of secular values of what is right or wrong, then it is a point of sowing the wind and reaping the whirlwind. That comes, in the end, in many forms: the warping of our own children's minds, the loss of values for them, the eternal drift they experience without a moral rudder to steer them, and the ultimate deterioration and decay of what is "light" and "salt" for an American society already full of cracks in the plaster.

The question of what to do about television is not for the secular minds alone to ponder. In fact, "Big Brother"—the entire galaxy of images that would control a population—is really the Goliath that belongs to the Christian Davids. It was so in biblical history and it is so today.

What this book attempts to do is to reach into the dormant nerve centers of the Christian and arouse him once again to the battle that must be waged. It is an attempt to disturb the complacent custodian of moral values—the Christian—and move him off his favorite TV chair to join that battle. It is not a question of throwing the baby out with the bath water. It is not simply a question of whether to build Christian TV stations to counter the influence of the secular ones. There is not enough time at this point in history to wait for that to emerge, assuming that such Christian TV stations could, in fact, hope to compete with the power of the networks. This is likewise not an appeal to shut off the TV, throw it out, or try some kind of deliberate censorship.

What this book is attempting to do is to confront the Christian with "Big Brother" as he is in his ugly, manipulative side and arouse a sleeping body of Christ to lay hold of the God-given resources to change it. In fact, if this book does nothing else but make the Christian more aware of what his children are viewing and what he himself is viewing—the ugly, sordid, denigrating garbage—then a big step has been taken in the right direction. It has been my pleasure to work with Gregg Lewis in his research and what he has written here. Few professors in writing have the privilege to work with a student who has proven himself to be both a master of prose and a disciplined analyst.

I am pleased to share his convictions on the subject and to be joined with him in this relationship of sounding a much-needed trumpet blast for the armies of the Lord, which have bivouacked far too long. The marching orders are here; the enemy is clearly in sight. God grant that this effort will bring the sound of chariots in the distance as the church militant rises once more to face the field of battle.

James L. Johnson

1
Big Brother Is Watching

Spring, 1977—The director of an Illinois preschool asked the parents of a new four-year-old student to fill out a standard information sheet about their son. After the question, "What name does your child want to be called?" the mother wrote, "The Fonz, or Steve Austin, the six-million-dollar man."

Winter, 1977—In an unprecedented scheduling strategy, ABC televised the eight-part saga of "Roots" on eight consecutive nights. The results were also unprecedented in television history. A staggering total of 130 million Americans followed part or all of Alex Haley's epic that traced his black slave-family's history from African freedom to new freedom at the end of the Civil War. When the series ended, millions of Americans followed Haley's example with a quest for their own family roots.

Genealogical libraries around the nation were flooded with inspired researchers. A month after "Roots" was aired, James J. Walker, genealogical specialist of the National Archives in Washington,

D.C., reported, "We have tripled the number of daily visitors. It has taxed our facilities to the point where we cannot accommodate them. A couple Saturdays ago we had a four-hour waiting line."[1]

Fall, 1976—In a national poll conducted by *Senior Scholastic Magazine*, American high-schoolers were asked, "Is there a man or woman living today who you consider your personal hero?" Top vote-getter was television's newest and biggest sex symbol, Farrah Fawcett-Majors.

In the first four months that her hit TV show, "Charlie's Angels," was on the air, "Farrah posters" became the hottest pop-art item in the country, with more than two million sold (smashing the previous poster record held by another TV star, "The Fonz").

Beauty shops across the country reported thousands of customers requesting the "Farrah look." The manager of a Chicago wig-making firm stated, "Our Farrah wigs have been our best sellers for weeks now."

After reading a fan magazine rumor about possible marital trouble between Farrah and her husband, one sixteen-year-old admirer from the Midwest saw his chance. He wrote and asked her to marry him if she ever got a divorce.

Fall, 1974—The nation's largest independent publisher of Sunday school materials was forced to introduce a totally new curriculum for preschoolers. The reason? "Sesame Street." The generation of preschoolers exposed to that television show were so advanced that teachers were finding the old curriculum obsolete.

Spring, 1973—An Atlanta television station broadcasted a movie called "The Marcus Nelson Murders." Just three weeks later, a young Atlanta woman was brutally raped and killed, her head bludgeoned and her throat cut. According to one of the homicide detectives investigating the case, the crime scene looked "exactly like the one on TV." A seventeen-year-old youth confessed he had reenacted the whole movie.

The evidence ranges from the humorous to the horrible. But the proof piles up. Television packs a walloping impact on our culture today.

Millions of lives are touched, or rather permeated, by TV on a daily basis. Recent A. C. Nielsen ratings show the television set in the average American home is on more than six hours a day. Preschoolers watch an average of 23.5 hours per week. Today's teen-ager will have logged at least 15,000 hours of viewing time by the time he graduates from high school—compared to an estimated 12,000 hours spent in school classrooms. Even many adult Americans devote more time to television viewing than to any activity except sleep and work.

But it is not just television's constant presence that makes it an influence on society. TV's very nature gives it an advantage over other media. Since watching doesn't demand the reading skill needed for books, magazines, or newspapers, TV precedes and often pre-empts the use of printed material. Television goes one-up on radio by showing as well as telling. Unlike movies, it runs continuously and penetrates nearly every home. Polls reveal that in nine of every ten homes, the set is located in the main sitting-around-in-the-evening room—either the living room or the family room. There, once purchased, it becomes a cheap, convenient, and almost unlimited source of family entertainment and information.

As a medium, TV is even unique in what it demands of the user. Printed material is taken at the reader's pace; a book can be put aside to be completed later. Radio activates the auditory system and often the imagination. But television calls for constant auditory and visual attention as it pulls the viewer along at its frantic pace. Except in the case of instant replays and late-season reruns, the viewer must get it the first time or not at all.

Media expert Tony Schwartz explains in *The Responsive Chord* that visualizing a television picture demands a unique neurological effort from the viewer. Unlike movies, which project a rapid succession of still pictures on the screen, a television's "picture" is only a series of electronically flashing dots.

The screen never shows a complete picture. To "see" an image on a television screen, the human eye must receive the stimulus from a few dots of light every millisecond. The eye transmits these impulses to the brain, which has to record them, recall the previous impulses, and predict future impulses in order for the mind to visualize the picture. The brain has to fill in or recall 99.999 percent of the image at any given moment. Since, as Schwartz points out, no previous human activity has ever demanded this kind of neurological involvement, much remains to be learned about the nature and effect of this physiological process.[2]

Big Brother Is Watching

The neurological and physiological effects of TV viewing aren't the only ones which aren't fully understood. Even though television has been a household phenomenon for years, the potential impact of the medium on civilization, society, and individual lives is still being hypothesized by researchers and social observers alike.

Most of us take television for granted; it has become an accepted and necessary part of our lives and our living rooms. We sit so close to our little screens that we don't see the big picture; we don't realize how much television has changed our culture.

Television has exploded the horizons of human experience. By the time today's children enter the first grade they have seen more of the world, have had more vicarious experiences, have been exposed to more sex and violence, have developed a larger listening vocabulary, and have become familiar with more commercial products than their grandparents did in a lifetime.[3]

At the same time, television has brought our whole nation closer together than a small town could have been a century ago. For while it has broadened individual perspectives, TV has also standardized our collective outlook and experience as a society. It has drawn a huge huddle of humanity into that small circle of glowing, phosphorescent light in front of the tube. And there, millions of Americans share the same excitements, the same disappointments, the same fears and hopes, and the same viewpoint of the same action unfolding on the screen.

The impact of this shared mass experience was summarized by Dr. George Gerbner, dean of the

University of Pennsylvania's Annenburg School of Communications and one of the nation's leading researchers on the subject, when he said, "Television has transformed the political life of the nation, has changed the daily habits of our people, has molded the style of the generation, made overnight global phenomena out of local happenings, and redirected the flow of information and values from traditional channels into centralized networks reaching into every home. In other words, it has profoundly affected . . . the process by which members of our species become human."[4]

For the Christian, Dr. Gerbner's comments should be especially alarming. He's saying that habits, attitudes, values—things that have traditionally been taught by parents, by the church, or by religious leaders—are now being taught by television. While the extent of TV's teaching and influence isn't known, this potential threat is something concerned Christians can't afford to ignore.

In recent years, a number of researchers have studied and documented various effects of television viewing. Most of the research has concentrated on the influence of violence and commercials on children, and almost all of it has been concerned with short-term effects. Yet the findings should arouse the concern of every Christian parent.

"One of the most disturbing effects of television appears to be the creation, in some people, of passivity," according to Harry J. Skornia, former president of the National Association of Educational Broadcasters.[5] He feels it would be impossible to measure the energy that television has drained away from other functions of society—education, civic, church, and family involvement.

The National Child Research Center (NCRC) in Washington, D.C. supports Skornia's belief. In a report filed in 1971 with the Federal Communications Commission, the NCRC charged: "Television represses children's innate tendencies because it requires passive rather than active involvement, and activity, not passivity, is necessary for children's full healthful development. . . ."[6]

Many critics accuse TV of isolating viewers, saying it hinders human relationships by robbing time which could be spent relating to parents, siblings, friends, and even strangers. They agree with T. S. Eliot's assessment that television is "a medium of entertainment which permits millions of people to listen to the same joke at the same time and yet remain lonesome."[7]

Television also affects viewers by what it teaches. Much of that is good. Over the years of its existence, TV has heightened awareness and broadened human knowledge.

Perhaps the best single example of TV's educational effectiveness is "Sesame Street." That one program drastically altered the lives of a whole generation of children. Not only has it effectively transmitted content learning such as verbal and numerical skills, the show has instilled attitudes and values such as cooperation, sharing, and brotherhood as well.

Unfortunately, not all of what is learned from television is planned or good. The action of the Atlanta teen who reenacted "The Marcus Nelson Murders" is only one extreme example. But behavioral scientists universally agree that people's values and behavior are largely shaped by observational learning. And since television plays such an integral part in modern American society, it has in many cases replaced friends, relatives, neighbors, and acquaintances as the model in observational learning. It is this role of television as an observational model that has created more alarm than any other factor of TV viewing.

The National Association for Better Broadcasting estimates that a child will see 13,000 violent television deaths between the ages of five and fifteen. The effects of such an onslaught of televised violence was the prime concern of a massive $1.8 million, three-year-long study conducted for the Surgeon General's Scientific Advisory Committee on Television and Social Behavior. Dr. Alberta Siegel, a noted psychologist and a member of this committee, testified to a Senate committee: "The substance of our report . . . and also of previous research was that there is now evidence for a causal link between watching TV violence and subsequent aggressive behavior by the viewer."[7]

Related studies indicate television not only influences viewer behavior, it can even alter the viewer's perception of reality. The University of Pennsylvania's Gerbner Report (1975) found that heavy viewers (those who watched four or more hours a day) are much more fearful of contemporary society than light viewers. For the heavy viewer, the overemphasis on fictional violence and crime on the screen was translated into increased fear of the real world. In other words, for a growing number in our television generation, the TV set doesn't just reflect reality; *it is reality*. The picture they get from their screens blurs and distorts their view of the real world around them.

Another of television's potent powers is its influence on decision-making. Advertisers realize it, even if viewers don't. In 1976, American business staked over $2.5 billion on its faith in prime-time network advertising. And they got results.

Surveys show that because of their exposure to advertising, children ask for specific brands. Their requests account for increased expenditures of an estimated $30 million a week (or $1.5 billion a year) in grocery retail sales alone. That doesn't include advertising's impact on adults or on anything but the food industry.

The decision-making influence of TV isn't confined to consumer choices. What should concern Christians even more is that for many viewers, television has become the yardstick against which they measure and make moral choices and on which they base their own attitudes and values. TV has become a major, if not the main, legitimizing agent in our society.

But until recently there has been little public concern about TV and its effects. Dr. Siegel states, "The American public has been preoccupied with governing our children's schooling. We have been astonishingly unconcerned about the medium that reaches into our homes. Yet we may expect television to alter our social arrangements just as profoundly as printing has done over the past five centuries."[8]

Then why the lack of concern for so long?

One reason might be the suddenness of the TV phenomenon. Within a generation of the creation of commercial television, more than 96 percent of American homes acquired sets. The medium entrenched itself in American life before the public had a chance to do any serious thinking about its effects.

An intriguing hypothesis for our lack of concern is proposed by Douglas Cater, director of the Aspen Institute's Program on Communication and Society. He points out scientific evidence that suggests thinking people are left-brained in development. They depend on the brain's left hemisphere—the portion that controls sequential, analytical tasks based on the use of propositional thought. TV appeals to the right hemisphere, which is non-sequential and non-analytical. So, Cater believes, the thinking person, or at least the thinking portion of his brain, is somewhat bewildered by television.[9]

Or perhaps our lack of concern about television is due to the natural human reluctance to question something "free"—something that's paid for by commercial advertisers. A careful inspection of the medium may seem tantamount to looking the proverbial gift horse in the mouth.

Whatever the reasons, Christian people have been just as guilty as the general public in ignoring the potential power of television. Of course, there's been the obligatory muttering about sex and violence on the tube. But most Christian families are as blindly addicted to their sets as the rest of society.

What traditionally has been the bastion of the church—the Christian family—has surrendered without a fight to what many experts feel is the most powerfully persuasive tool mankind has ever known. Every night after supper, the set comes on and the typical Christian family plops down to relax, enjoy, and share the same vicarious experiences as their non-Christian neighbors. Every night that family is sucked into the mainstream of secular thought, attitudes, and values. Seldom is there a family discussion or even a parental thought as to how the action on the screen contradicts the biblical norms by which Christians should live.

Christian parents often take the attitude that "Television doesn't affect our family. Maybe non-Christians, but not us. Any possible bad effects are more than offset by our regular Christian input."

But that rationale can't stand up to the sheer weight of the odds. An average person today who follows the typical viewing pattern will spend the equivalent of more than nine years in front of the TV set by the time he or she is sixty-five. If the same person goes to Sunday school every week during those years, he will receive little more than four months' worth of Christian education. And as noted Christian educator and communicator Joseph T. Bayly wrote: "Even if TV were morally neutral, it would have serious effects on Christian life and thought. You don't spend nine years of life watching anything without being affected by it. Or even six or seven years."[10]

A shocking number of Christian parents seem to have given up any hope of controlling TV's effects on their children. Thirty-six percent of the parents polled in one midwestern church know for its tradition of strong evangelicalism admitted that their own children were probably adopting new attitudes about sex, violence, and virtue in general. Yet they felt, "It's far worse to hassle them about it than to allow them the exposure."

With that sort of attitude, it's not surprising that more and more Christian households now sport at least two TV sets—one for mom and dad and one for the kids. So while son and daughter gawk and grin at the snide and often raw sex of the "socially relevant" situation comedies, mom and dad are tripping back nostalgia alley with "The Waltons" or "Little House on the Prairie."

Separate lives with separate moral values are being developed under the same roof. Not every child or teen takes behavioral cues from the TV set, of course, but a steady diet of secular values and viewpoints can't help but raise a young person's tolerance and acceptance levels. This could even be one explanation for why so many people from Christian families are growing restless with the spiritual virtues, values, and behavior expected by their parents and their churches.

Certainly television shouldn't receive sole blame for the spiritual erosion in today's society. But in light of the research results concerning TV's effect on perception, attitudes, and behavior, it would be foolish to continue to ignore its threat.

Fortunately, the climate of concern is changing. Christians and the general public alike are re-examining the television medium.

The national Parent-Teacher Association (PTA) has launched a storm of protest aimed primarily at the violence-laced content of network television. On June 30, 1976, the American Medical Association's House of Delegates approved a resolution that called for all physicians to protest televised violence and to oppose the sponsors of the most violent shows. A number of religious groups and denominations have also jumped into the action.

Even the J. Walter Thompson Agency, one of the biggest and most influential voices in American advertising, has expressed concern. The agency has called for an examination of the effects of televised sex and violence and is steering its clients away from offensive shows.

This new popular outcry, combined with mounting reams of research, is creating a real dilemma for concerned Christian parents. They realize they can't continue to deny TV's effect on their own lives and on the lives of their families. They understand the power of the picture.

Yet they're realistic enough to know there are no easy solutions. Banning the tube from Christian homes is a poor alternative; all the potential benefits are lost along with the bad effects. A barrage of critical attacks and righteous condemnation isn't likely to redeem or convert the massive television industry.

Then what can be done?

Concerned Christians are going to have to struggle with the television issue. They are going to have to carefully consider and choose appropriate Christian attitudes, actions, and reactions to television—for themselves and for their families. To do that, they're going to have to answer some difficult questions.

Just what does television teach the viewer? What can be done to enhance any positive effects of TV? What can and should be done to negate or alter the negative effects? How is television's influence on Christians different from its impact on other viewers? What role should parents play in controlling the medium? How could Christians best use television? What alternative strategies should individual Christians or the Christian community adopt in response to television's impact?

Not all these questions can be conclusively answered at present. But there is enough evidence available to get a good start. That can be the first step in mastering the medium of television.

2
Big Brother
Is Being Watched

In 1954, a leading Christian magazine offered the following criticism of the fairly new medium of television.

By the mere flick of the dial the living room of the Christian home now may be transformed instantly into a theater, night club, or wrestling arena. Tens of thousands of Christians who previously lived cloistered lives and never saw the inside of a nightclub may now sit at the table next to the floor show without leaving their homes. Many to whom a wrestling match was but recently a vulgar exhibition not enjoyed by respectable people, now discuss freely the attributes of Gorgeous George. The struggle Christians are experiencing is plainly revealed.[1]

In 1975, a leading secular magazine printed an article criticizing television and cited the following case.

TELEGARBAGE

On September 10, 1974, at 8 p.m., NBC aired "Born Innocent," a drama about a juvenile detention home in which a gang of inmates corner a young girl in a shower and sexually violate her with a plumber's tool. Four days later, near San Francisco, four children, ages 9 to 15, seized two little girls on a public beach and replayed the scene with beer bottles. Three of the perpetrators told the police they had seen the "Born Innocent" telecast.[2]

The first criticism seems mild, or perhaps naive, in contrast to the shocking influence the made-for-TV movie "Born Innocent" had on the four San Francisco juveniles who reenacted what they saw. The difference between the two indictments reveals how much television changed in those twenty-one years.

Yet the underlying warning is the same. Both magazines were insisting that television can and does affect viewers.

At television's outset, few if any people recognized its potential for influencing society. In fact, the new medium met with widespread skepticism when it was introduced to the public by RCA at the 1939 World's Fair in New York City. A reporter for the *New York Times* concluded: "The problem with television is that people must sit and keep their eyes glued on the screen; the average American family hasn't time for it. Therefore, the showmen are convinced that for this reason, if for no other, television will never be a serious competitor of broadcasting."[3]

That reporter could never have imagined how ridiculous his evaluation would seem today. But there were few if any people in 1939 who could have guessed how the whole television industry would mushroom.

Commercial television actually began in the United States when Congress authorized stations to begin program tests on July 1, 1941. But regular commercial broadcasting didn't get launched until after World War II, when in 1946 a total of six stations served an audience of 8,000 families. By 1949 only 2.3 percent of American homes had sets; however, the beachhead was established and the invasion was on.

In 1950, Dr. Edward Carnell, in what was perhaps the first serious look at television from a Christian perspective, wrote, "Not long ago we smiled rather skeptically when men of science prophesied that within our own generation every home would be a theater. Such fantasies appeared no more likely a fulfillment than does a round-trip excursion to the moon today."[4]

But by 1950 it was evident that the scientists' prophecies would come true. Within five years, more than half of all American homes had TVs. And only seventeen years after Dr. Carnell recognized a fantasy becoming reality, the "theaters" in the homes of more than 94 percent of American families gave them a bird's-eye view of that first "round-trip excursion to the moon."

Today, the communications invasion that began three decades ago might be better described as a full-scale occupation. Recent Nielsen surveys show that more than 96 percent of American homes have at least one set. Over 40 percent have more than one.

Perhaps, as the *Times* correspondent suggested, the average American family didn't have time for television in 1939. But Americans soon made time for it; they actually restructured family life to do so. Sixty percent of the families studied in the early 1960s by a Brooklyn College sociologist had changed their sleeping patterns because of TV. Fifty-five percent had altered eating schedules and 78 percent used television as an "electric" baby-sitter.[5] But perhaps the most poignant proof of TV's intrusion into home and personal life is that water-systems engineers now must design city water-supply systems to accommodate the inevitable drop in water pressure caused by mass toilet flushing during prime-time television commercials.

Before television gained such widespread popularity and use, some Christians saw real potential for good. A few dreamers envisioned it as a powerful tool of mass evangelism. Other Christians, like many secular communicators, foresaw TV's great educational and informational potential.

But many Christians viewed the new medium as a potential threat to them and their families. Dr. Carnell summarized the potential dangers he saw into four threats: (1) The threat of secularization of our culture if television "spreads the delusion that the whole man can find full satisfaction without serious reference to God." (2) The threat of destroying personal initiative. (3) The threat posed by "the temptation to exploit fleshly lust." (4) The threat to children.[6]

Almost all of today's criticism of television could be lumped into one of Carnell's four categories. Although potential problems of television still fit the same basic pattern after nearly thirty years, Christian attitudes and actions in regard to the medium have changed dramatically.

In the earliest years of television, many Christians settled the TV issue simply by not owning a set. But that strategy was destined to failure. By 1953, half the evangelicals surveyed by *Moody Monthly* reportedly owned TVs.[7] That was approximately the same percentage of ownership found in the general public.

Despite the growing acceptance of TV ownership among Christians, some strong opposition remained. As one former hard-liner remembered his cohorts, "We were sort of anti-television vigilantes shooting TV antennas off roofs. Oh, we didn't actually use guns," he explained. "We'd just ride around our neighborhoods checking rooftops. If we spotted an antenna on the home of one of our church members, we'd stop and pray with them about their problem."

Such tactics created a lot of guilt and often prompted evasive action. One minister recalled an example from the fifties. "I was visiting in a parishioner's home one evening," he said. "The man opened his closet to hang up my coat and about died of embarrassment when I noticed the little nine-inch television set that had been hidden in the closet before my arrival.

"But it seemed like the most popular television for Christians was the kind that closed like a cabinet in the front," he went on. "That way a visitor wouldn't even know it was a TV unless he walked over and opened the doors. It meant you didn't have to bother hiding it in the closet before the minister showed up."

According to the response on the 1953 *Moody Monthly* survey, most of those Christians who did own TVs said their concern about the potential harm of television prompted strict regulation of the viewing in their families. Some even sought outside help in their struggle to decide how to regulate their viewing.

"I remember," said one minister who pastored an inner-city church at the time, "when members of my congregation would come to me with their *TV Guide* and ask if I'd pick out the programs their family ought to watch during the next week."

Yet even with the concern over the regulation of viewing, *Moody Monthly* reported in the summary of its survey:

> One of the striking aspects of the survey was the indication that TV sets in Christian homes are often turned on for several hours a day. Even those seeking to control the length of viewing time or types of programs reported their sets are in operation for perhaps an average of two to four hours a day. This indicates that probably no single activity in the waking day consumes as much time as television viewing."[8]

Perhaps the television dilemma for the Christians of the fifties was best summarized by the statement, "Replies to the questionnaires estimate that Christians are groping for a more satisfactory method of dealing with TV and related issues."[9]

If indeed the Christians of the fifties seemed to struggle with their relationship to television, those of the sixties seemed to accept it with few reservations. In fact, it wasn't at all unusual for pastors to recognize television's pull by announcing evening services with the added encouragement, "We'll be done in time for everyone to get home for 'Bonanza.'"

Perhaps Christians' acceptance of TV in the sixties was only a reflection of a growing addiction on the part of the general population. The National Association of Broadcasters' figures show that daily exposure of TV in the average home continued to rise during that decade—from five hours and three minutes in 1960 to a daily turned-on time of five hours and fifty-six minutes by the end of the decade.

Another factor in TV's acceptance by Christians may have been the respect it gained. Dr. Robert T. Bower's research through the Roper organization showed that during the sixties TV passed radio, newspapers, and magazines to become the medium the public rated most entertaining, most educational, most interest-creating, and most politically informative. It also became the medium that "did the most for the public."[10]

According to Bower's study, the sixties saw a marked change in the perceived role of TV in the home. In 1960, the "baby-sitting" function of TV was seen as the second-greatest advantage of TV for children. By 1970, parents saw TV primarily as an educator for their children.[11] So it could be that this new, loftier role of television helped it gain acceptance from Christian parents.

Whatever the reasons, Christian attitudes and reactions did change. A quick look through the Christian literature of the sixties proves it. Some

Christians were still talking about how to best use their televisions, but they were no longer debating whether or not to own a set.

In fact, TV ownership had become so prevalent by the mid-sixties that *Moody Monthly* wrote:

> The local church is undoubtedly affected in a definite way by TV competition. Many believe that excessive Saturday night viewing makes an appreciable difference in attendance at Sunday School and church on Sunday morning. Certainly the Sunday evening service finds itself competing with one of the most glittering entertainment arrays of the week. Midweek activities likewise suffer from the pull of the easy chair and the television set.[12]

But during the sixties, when Christians limited their criticism to television's competition with the church programs, a few serious researchers began questioning the harmful psychological effects television viewing might have on children. The Surgeon General's Scientific Advisory Committee launched its massive study of television and social behavior. And even before that, concerned parents and professionals formed local and national action groups like Action for Children's Television to try to counter the harm they felt TV was inflicting on children. Yet Christians and the church were strangely silent.

Joseph Bayly chided the Christian community for its lack of concern when he wrote:

> As we enter the 70's, psychologists have become our consciences in areas of human behavior. Warnings about the effects of TV-watching are coming

from psychiatrists and educators—not from pastors. The Church has apparently defaulted on its responsibility in favor of the psychologist. Whatever threat pastors see in television is not related to its effect on the human mind and behavior, but the effect on Sunday evening church attendance and pastoral home visitation.[13]

So far, the Christian response to television in the seventies seems to be a continuation of the simple acceptance of the sixties. There have been some exceptions: occasional news reports mention irate ministers who lead their congregations in TV-burning bonfire ceremonies; a few denominational commissions have sponsored hearings; and a number of concerned Christians have tried to mount letter-writing campaigns and organized protests such as "Turn Off the Television Week." But the daily turned-on time of the television set in the average Christian home continues to rise. Very few believers seem to be struggling with the TV issue today.

Yet, while the average Christian's attitude toward the medium has remained static, television has changed drastically in the seventies. Like society, TV has experienced a revolution in basic values. Some would claim television should take a large part of the blame—that it has actually introduced a new set of values. Others would say TV only reflects the values that already exist in society. There are strong points for both views. So the argument, like the one about the order of appearance of the chicken and the egg, could drone on forever.

What can't be argued is that there has been a

values revolution. And whether television is cause, effect, or a little bit of both, it's definitely a part of the action. With the onslaught of "socially relevant" sit-coms, Christians laughed and smiled their way to increased acceptance, or at least tolerance, of promiscuity, homosexuality, and even abortion. An increasing number of explicit television presentations now "warn" viewers with the further enticement: "Due to mature subject matter, parental discretion is advised."

But parental discretion, even among Christian parents, is often lacking. The sweeping changes of the seventies seem to have ambushed them with a whole new set of values they don't understand and feel helpless to resist.

The finger of blame could be pointed any number of ways. This values dilemma could be traced to a "permissive society" syndrome which many Christians adopted without a whimper. It could be traced to a lack of strong preaching from American pulpits on the subject of character and personal "righteousness." Or the problem could be blamed on a future shock that has paralyzed the church's prophetic vocal chords and prevented the Christian establishment from preparing its people to grapple with the real issues of our present society.

Whatever the roots of the problem, the sweeping seventies are here. They've been here for years. And their presence is being experienced in Christian homes—primarily through the channel of television. The question is: What can be done about TV now as we approach the 1980s?

Christians today face several alternatives. They

can continue the silence of the sixties and early seventies. They can return to the condemnation and the criticism of the fifties. Or they can take a careful look at TV's effect on viewers and take a fresh, new stance based on consistent Christian principles.

This last choice demands a closer look at recent research and the findings those studies have turned up about television and some of its alarming effects on viewers.

3
Mayhem in the P.M.:
The Behavior Transfer

On September 30, 1973, ABC broadcasted the movie "Fuzz" as its "Sunday Night Movie." The film portrayed a gang of delinquents who doused waterfront derelicts with gasoline and set them afire—just for kicks.

Two days later, twenty-five-year-old Evelyn Wagler ran out of gas while driving through a Boston slum. She walked to a nearby gas station and was returning with a can of gas when six young men surrounded her. They dragged her into a vacant lot, beat her, and ordered her to pour the gasoline over herself. Then they set her on fire and left her screaming and rolling in the dirt. Evelyn Wagler died a few hours later.

In Miami, three weeks after the Boston burning, four junior-high boys, including one who had seen the "Fuzz" telecast, stole some lighter fluid. Then, "They doused three winoes sleeping behind a vacant building, ignited a match and laughed hilariously as the men woke screaming, running, and beating the flames. One died of his burns."[1]

On February 26, 1974, NBC broadcasted a "Police Story" in which actor Jackie Cooper played a sadistic ex-con who committed a series of rapes and murders during a string of bar and liquor-store holdups.

Two weeks later, the March 12 issue of the *New York Daily News* printed an article that read:

> A gypsy cab driver accused of killing three persons in a Queens bar stickup told detectives after his arrest that he got the idea for the robbery from a TV crime show, police disclosed yesterday.
>
> Homicide detectives said the suspect, Richard Schroeck, 29, told them he planned the holdup after watching a February 26 drama described in an advertisement as "A supercharged Police Story special."
>
> Police said Schroeck entered the bar around 1 a.m. Monday and drank quietly until 3:15 when he was told the place was closing. Then he allegedly pulled a gun and held up the two couples who were the only people in the bar. Police say he forced them to the rear and made the two women remove their clothes.
>
> Detectives said he apparently planned to follow the "Police Story" script and sexually assault at least one of the women, but they resisted his advances so he started shooting. He allegedly shot the men first, then the women, and finally stabbed the women with two steak knives.[2]

While incidents like these are certainly shocking, they unfortunately are no longer surprising. They are but three of the numerous, widely publicized

examples of televised violence that have been tragically replayed in real life.

> During the last decade, two national violence
> commissions and an overwhelming number of scien-
> tific studies have continually come to one conclu-
> sion: televised and filmed violence can powerfully
> teach, suggest—even legitimize—extreme antisocial
> behavior, and can in some viewers trigger specific
> aggressive or violent behavior. The research of many
> behavioral scientists has shown that the definite
> cause-effect relationship exists between violence on
> TV and violent behavior in real life.[3]

Much of the concern about the effects of televised
violence is due to sensational cases such as the ones
in Boston, Miami, and New York. But the very prevalence of violence on television has invited the attention of the public and the researcher alike.

Murder and mayhem are the main movers and
motivators of action on prime-time television. Recent reports have shown what should come as no
surprise to even the most casual viewer: eight out of
ten programs contain violence.

The murder figures are the most familiar. Whether
the average American child will see more than 11,000
TV killings by the age of fourteen, more then 13,000
between ages five and fifteen, or just an average of a
thousand or so murders a year (depending on whose
estimates you use), the statistics are staggering.

Combine the mayhem with the murder, and the
total violence figures are almost beyond comprehen-
sion. Dr. Victor B. Cline, a noted researcher and

psychologist, found in one recent survey that during a single week of television the different channels in one large city showed 7,887 acts of violence and 1,087 threats of violence (such as "I'll break your legs!").[4]

This glut of gore on the tube drew special concern in the late sixties after the assassinations of the two Kennedys and Martin Luther King, Jr. Partially as a result of subsequent vocal public concern, more extensive research has been done in recent years on the effects of TV violence than on any other aspect of the medium.

"The most convincing research we have about TV's effects," wrote Alberta Siegel, a member of the Surgeon General's Scientific Advisory Committee on Television and Social Behavior, "is the research showing that televised persons provide an example or a model for the viewer's behavior."[5]

Agreeing that "there are now numerous documented instances of direct imitation of TV violence by children, which have been truly unfortunate," Drs. Robert M. Liebert, Emily S. Davidson, and John M. Neale, in a joint paper on aggression in childhood, cited two cases.

One young boy was stabbed while he and his friends reenacted scenes they had just seen from a rerun movie, "Rebel Without a Cause." Another youngster laced the family dinner with ground glass after observing it done on a crime show.[6]

Children aren't the only ones who imitate violent TV behavior. On December 13, 1966, NBC presented the drama "The Doomsday Flight." The plot revolved around a bomb placed on a plane and set to go off when the plane descended to a certain altitude.

Mayhem in the P.M.: The Behavior Transfer

The plane was saved when the pilot landed at a mountain airport above the altitude the bomb was rigged for.

While the movie was still on, one U.S. airline received a bomb threat. Within twenty-four hours, four more were phoned in. Within the next week, eight such hoax calls were received by various airlines. The Federal Aviation Agency blamed "The Doomsday Flight" for this rash of bomb threats equaling the number of calls for the entire previous month.[7]

Grant H. Hendrick, a prisoner serving a life sentence in Michigan's Marquette maximum security prison, insists TV is actually a school for criminals. He interviewed 208 of his fellow inmates and found that nine of every ten inmates had learned new tricks and improved their criminal techniques by watching TV. Four out of ten admitted copying specific television crimes.[8]

One thirty-four-year-old inmate who had spent fifteen years of his life behind bars claimed:

> TV has taught me how to steal cars, how to break into establishments, how to go about robbing people, even how to roll a drunk. Once, after watching a "Hawaii Five-O" episode, I robbed a gas station. The show showed me how to do it. Nowadays [he's serving a term for attempted rape] I watch TV in my house [cell] from 4 p.m. until midnight. I just sit back and take notes . . .I tell myself that I'll do it the same way when I get out. You could probably pick any 10 guys in here and ask 'em and they'd tell you the same thing. Everybody's picking up what's on the TV.[9]

47

The case for the effect of televised violence on behavior doesn't rest solely on the words of criminals or on the numerous documented examples. Laboratory studies also offer convincing results. One experiment carried out by three researchers at the University of North Carolina's Child Development Center revealed that once-a-day exposure to regular Saturday morning programs, over eleven different days, resulted in an increase in interpersonal aggression. In some youngsters, aggressiveness increased 200 to 300 percent.[10]

Many Christian parents look at experiments like this and read all the newspaper accounts of crime and violence copied from TV and think, "That's awful. But our kids are good kids—not criminals. Sure, TV violence is bad, but our family has strong biblical, Christian guidelines for behavior." But even a strong dose of faith doesn't guarantee immunity.

Liebert, Davidson and Neale said:

> More than fifty studies have been concluded, involving more than 10,000 children from every type of background. With remarkable consistency, the studies regularly lead to one conclusion: there is a clear and reliable relationship between the amount of violence which a child sees on entertainment television and the degree to which he is aggressive in his attitudes and behavior.[11]

Often, behavior is learned without being acted out until a suitable situation arises. Widely quoted experiments conducted by Stanford psychologist Albert Bandura have shown that even brief exposure to novel aggressive behavior can be repeated in free play by as many as 88 percent of the young children seeing it on TV. He also demonstrated that the behavior could be recalled and reproduced by children for as long as six months later after only a single exposure.[12] In other words, if the right situation presents itself, children can and often will respond with aggressive behavior modeled after action they have seen on television.

It is true that the laboratory studies have not specifically shown how children in Christian homes have been affected by TV violence. But Christian parents who discount the likelihood of their children copying TV violence might look at some other possible effects. Overt behavioral response may be only one effect of violent television content.

Exposure to a violent diet of TV may also affect attitudes. The message conveyed by so many television programs is that violence and aggression are viable solutions to many conflicts. Even if viewers don't apply that thinking to their own lives and problems, it at least raises their tolerance of that attitude in others.

In fact, research by Dr. Cline and others indicates that as viewers experience violent episode after violent episode without any chance for constructive reaction or interference, they learn a conditioned non-response. They become gradually desensitized to the sight of violence.

That research is supported by a recent poll of junior-high teens conducted by the Encyclopedia Britannica Educational Corporation. More than 90 percent of the 2,000 youths surveyed stated they "did not find TV violence objectionable."[13]

But what is even more frightening is that this tolerance of TV violence can be transferred to real-life situations. In an experiment conducted by two researchers at the Florida Technological University at Orlando, forty-four third-and fourth-graders were asked to "supervise" two preschoolers by means of a closed-circuit television. A tape of a progressively violent fight between the preschoolers was fed into the closed-circuit system. Children who had just been shown a fifteen-minute excerpt from an actual detective show took significantly longer to summon adult help than did children who did not see the violent program segment.[14]

These and other findings prompted the two experimenters, Ronald Drabman and Margaret Hanratty Thomas, to conclude:

> While the exact psychological mechanism remains to be discovered, the over-all conclusion is frightening. It is even more chilling when one combines this new data with the older modeling research. TV violence may be having the dual effect of exacerbating some children's violent behavior while at the same time teaching the rest to tolerate their aggression. A future society in which virtually all adults have been exposed to a continued deluge of violence since infancy could well be an unfortunate place to live.[15]

The effects may reach even those parents concerned enough to take measures to shelter themselves and their children from the flood of televised violence. For even when children are not exposed to a large amount of violent programming, they can become the target of aggression, the victim of some child who is stimulated by the anti-social violence and aggression he sees on the tube.

If the potential hazards of violence are so well known, why hasn't something been done?

One reason might have been the popular notion that violence on television could be beneficial. For a long time many behavioral scientists believed TV violence acted as a catharsis by draining aggressive tendencies from some people. But in recent years most experts have abandoned that thinking.

Of course, the big reason for the continued violence is the networks' reluctance to change. In their research for the Surgeon General's report, Thomas Baldwin and Colby Lewis examined the industry's own view of violence; they found it excused with a variety of arguments.

Television people often claimed they were just reflecting life—that life was violent. But critics counter this by pointing to TV's overemphasis on crime and violence; they argue that television presents a distorted reflection.

Some defenders of the medium argued that violence has always played a large part in all literature and drama throughout history—from the Bible on down. But Dr. Rex C. Ramsey, director of the Arkansas Department of Health, challenged that excuse. He admitted, "Violence and aggression have always been a part of our children's lives. Fairy tales and bedtime stories with violence have been with us as long as the 'Red Riding Hood.' " But he went on to say, "The difference is the person telling the story, the time to explain and answer questions and the most important thing is that the person doing the violent act was not successful in the old fairy tales."[16] It may also be added that before the existence of television, violence was never presented in living color; neither has literature, drama, nor even the Bible been consumed in the continuous hour-after-hour quantities that TV is in the average home today.

One of the reasons for so much violence, but one which TV people are understandably reluctant to admit, is that violence is easy. Action-adventure series have dominated television since the mid-fifties. Plot problems can be easily solved just by catching or killing someone. Writers merely vary the same old formula. It's much easier than grappling with real, complicated social problems.

But perhaps the most telling argument the television industry offers for the continued prevalence of violence is that it is just providing what the public wants. Despite a recent poll by the Opinion Research Corporation of Princeton, N.J., that found 71 percent of the American public saying they think there is too much violence on TV, more people are watching more television than ever before.[17] What shocked us yesterday doesn't shock us today, and so the violence scale keeps right on escalating.

Maybe the overall acceptance of violence shouldn't be surprising at all. Dr. Walter Menninger, senior staff psychiatrist of the Menninger Foundation, explained that violence is fascinating. "The aggressive emotional drive is present within all of us. . . . It remains a powerful force within."[18] Christians especially, with their understanding of human capability for sin and evil, should understand Dr.

Menninger's evaluation. They should realize the basis for the public's mixed feeling about violence. Yet despite people's acceptance and even enjoyment of violent entertainment, the TV industry can't be absolved of all wrongdoing. The indictment made by the Eisenhower Commission on Violence still stands. That special presidential commission concluded in its summary report, "Television entertainment based on violence may be effective merchandising, but it is an appalling way to serve a civilization—an appalling way to fulfill the requirements of law that broadcasts serve 'public interest, convenience, and necessity.' "[19]

Dr. Siegel underscored the seriousness of the TV violence issue when she summarized the Surgeon General's report. She testified before the Senate's Subcommittee on Communications:

> My own guess is that TV violence has negative effects on all child viewers, but that countervailing forces overcome these effects in the majority. In the minority, the positive influences in their lives are not sufficient to counteract the baneful effects of hours of watching aggressive modes of conflict resolution. The result is that the children adopt these aggressive modes in their own lives. When we talk about a minority of American children, it is important to remember that we are talking about millions of children. . . . They need our concern.[20]

U.S. Surgeon General Jess Steinfeld told the same Senate subcommittee:

> It is important to keep in mind that anti-social behavior existed in our society long before television

appeared. We must be careful not to make television programming the whipping boy for all society's ills. Yet we must take whatever actions we can when we do identify factors contributing to anti-social behavior in our society. . . . There comes a time when the data are sufficient to justify action. That time has come.[21]

The question is: What action can be taken?

In the fall of 1975, the networks (with the encouragement of the Federal Communications Commission) adopted plans for a "Family Hour." The idea was to reduce the amount of violence and sex in prime-time programming—before 9:00 P.M. (8:00 P.M. Central Time)—the hours when the most children are viewing.

Eventually a federal judge ruled the "Family Hour" concept unconstitutional, but by then its effectiveness was already questionable. Nielsen ratings showed that millions of children were watching beyond the "Family Hour" time slot. And the 1976 Gerbner Report on violent content in programming indicated that an increase of crime at the later hours had in effect raised, not lowered, the overall violent content. The rate of violent episodes was up to 5.6 per program, the highest rate on record.

So far, the industry's attempt to police itself has been rather anemic. Of course, network spokesmen periodically claim a reduction in violence, and the 1976–77 season did see a sizable drop in the number of action-adventure shows. But critics point to what is left, count the crimes, and continue to charge the networks with victimizing their viewers.

Mayhem in the P.M.: The Behavior Transfer

With a number of groups such as the PTA and the AMA spotlighting the problem, there is a growing public cry for an end to television violence. But there isn't an easy "all-or-nothing" solution. Many difficult questions demand answers.

Just what is violence? Is a slapstick comedian's kick in the pants as detrimental to viewers as a brutal shooting or stabbing? (Some violence scales count both as equally "aggressive acts.") Where do you draw the line? When is violence legitimate? Is it more permissible to depict Captain Ahab being killed by Moby Dick than it is to show Starsky and Hutch shooting a rapist? If there are "too many" murders on television, how many would be permissible? Such questions complicate what at first seems like such a clearly defined issue.

For Christians who are trying to evaluate and decide their own attitudes and actions with regard to television, the findings on the violence issue have to be weighed. But before charting a definite course through the television dilemma, Christians need to consider other influences of the medium as well. If television violence can be the effective teacher of actions and attitudes that the evidence seems to indicate, Christians need to consider other TV content and discover what else television teaches.

4
Sex in the Script

The subject of sex may actually surpass mayhem in total tube time and script line count. Yet it has attracted little serious study. While television violence and its effects have been tabulated, tested, and protested by untold researchers, educators, and parents, the screen's plethora of permissiveness and promiscuity has been pretty much ignored and accepted as a natural outgrowth of today's society. Few people even seem willing to point a finger of shame for fear of being labeled some sort of Puritan prude.

Yet if the overemphasis of TV violence can affect the mind, the attitudes, and the behavior of viewers to the extent research suggests, then the tube treatment of sex may have equally serious implications. For sex saturates the set.

On October 4, 1976, a sleazily suggestive newspaper ad that appeared in papers across the country exhorted TV viewers to turn on "Executive Suite" and "meet the Porno Queen who brought a corporation to its knees." Another ad for the show promised: "Fresh disclosures of a beauty's sordid fling in porno pix pose a deep threat to the career of the man she loves."

That same week the same network offered the following shows:

"All's Fair"—A *TV Guide* ad described this show, "An invitation to a bachelor pad for a cozy dinner for two has Charley worried that she's going to be the main dish."

"Rhoda"—A newspaper ad said, "Swinging bachelor moves into Rhoda's pad! It's strictly a business deal. Or so the man says!" Of course, it wasn't long until Rhoda discovered he was interested in more than economic convenience.

"Maude"—Mrs. Naugatuck decided to have her elderly boyfriend live with her. Newspapers advertised the show with the blurb, "Maude vetoes live-in maid's live-in boyfriend."

"One Day at a Time"—In the middle of a four-episode story, teen-aged Julie and her boyfriend ran away and shacked up in a van.

"Good Times"—One of his sister's good-looking teachers, an ad said, "offers to teach J.J. the facts of life."

"Phyllis"—A description stated that Phyllis is "at a loss for words when her daughter asks her advice on matters pertaining to birth control."

This sampling of sex from just a few of the CBS series, plus the fact that the network had suffered a surprise, early-season rating slump, prompted *Chicago Tribune* critic Gary Deeb to charge that the network's solution for attracting more viewers "appears to be a combination of advertising innuendo and exploitative programs."[1]

Lou Dorfsman, CBS vice-president for corporate advertising, claimed that just wasn't so. He insisted, "We are not making a concerted effort to be vulgar. It looks a hell of a lot worse than it is. We're just playing it loose in a very contemporary sort of way."[2]

"Loose" is certainly an apt description of television's usual attitude toward sex. Those CBS shows were only typical. Deeb's disgust could just as eaily have been aimed at any week on any network.

Of course, sexual inferences and innuendos have played a part in television entertainment since vaudevillian burlesque antics in the industry's early days. And in some ways the treatment of sex has always been a contemporary reflection of societal standards.

Fifties television, in keeping with existing views on the privacy of sex, was carefully circumspect. Bedroom scenes, if shown at all on the family comedies, involved long pajamas and twin beds for husband and wife. Sex was denied more than suggested. But by the coming of the Bicentennial and the sexual revolution, things were different on TV. Marital status didn't matter. Underwear wasn't uncommon. Every single girl needed a double bed. And far from denying the existence of sex, "Mary Hartman, Mary Hartman" and her husband lay in bed and discussed his impotence.

Such openness and candor is common in the sexually liberated seventies. So the industry's claims of "just being contemporary" has some truth. But a number of shows seem to dredge even deeper than the low norms of a permissive society. "Mary Hartman, Mary Hartman" is a prime example. The absurdities and the shock tactics of this soap-opera spoof made it an overnight phenomenon. Its exploitation of sexual themes was evidenced by a *Newsweek* cover story description: "Most of the action takes place in the Hartman's squeaky-clean kitchen. There, when not fretting over the 'waxy yellow buildup' on her floor, Mary grapples with the horrors of marijuana and masturbation, venereal disease, fraudulent faith healers, open marriages, and a neighborhood mass murder triggered by a bad 'knock knock' joke."[3]

That description didn't mention the four weeks' worth of episodes about Mary's husband's impotence and their experience with a sex surrogate; or the neighbor who describes her sexual fulfillment in detail and whose husband is shot in the groin and has to have television's first testicle transplant; or Mary's promiscuous sister and her trouble as a massage-parlor hostess; or Mary's parents who are having trouble because her father patronized a prostitute; or Mary's puberty-aged daughter who constantly comments on her menstrual cramps and what she thinks may be her stunted sexual development; or Mary's grandpa who is better known to the local police department as "the Fernwood Flasher" due to his continuous indecent exhibitionism. This and other sordid action all took place during the first twenty-six weeks of the show.

This kind of treatment of previously taboo topics plus increasingly explicit prime-time sexual themes

Sex in the Script

and scenes prompted *New York Times* television reviewer John J. O'Connor to recognize "an increasing amount of program material verging on the pornographic—nothing beyond the amorphous range of soft core, mind you, but unmistakably pornographic nevertheless."

O'Connor went on to say:

> The porn development is new, at least for the carefully monitored hours of evening prime time. In fact, as is known by any lawyer or by any theater operator showing 'adult' movies, it is virtually impossible to define pornography, especially in an era noted for its new permissiveness. But the court definition of 'an appeal to prurient interest' will do as well as any other. In hard core, that appeal is direct and explicit. Soft core can be merely suggestive to varying degrees. And . . . television thrives on the power of suggestion.[4]

A casual survey of a smattering of shows makes TV's appeal to prurient interests glaringly obvious. Why else do so many of TV's women cops work undercover posing as prostitutes in order to get information? Why else would "Charlie's Angels" conduct their investigations in so many different revealing costumes every week? Or why do so many TV stars spend more time bathing and getting dressed than doing many normally more time-consuming activities. (One suspects that if TV heroines spent half as much time reading as they do in the shower, the nation's libraries might soon be overcrowded and Hollywood's contribution to water conservation would go a long way toward world drought relief.)

TELEGARBAGE

Sometimes the appeal is far from subtle. It can be embarrassingly plain to a viewer sitting in a roomful of people watching something as blatantly suggestive as the episode of "Switch" aired in the popular family viewing-time slot on Sunday evening, March 27, 1977.

During one scene in that show, Linda Day George, playing a sensual French ballet dancer, snuggled up to Robert Wagner and tried to seduce him with an enticing claim that a dancer's body was specially trained so that every muscle would do what she wanted it to. Of course, the whole time she was saying this and more, Wagner responded with his coyest smile of acceptance and anticipation. Though nothing more than a backrub transpired, the appeal to prurient interests was undeniable. Yet the scene was only a little more suggestive than many similar situations on other programs.

For some reason—perhaps guilt—the networks sometimes attempt to conceal their most sordid exploitations of sex with the flimsiest, see-through disguises. *New York Times* TV critic O'Connor cited one of these when he wrote:

> Recently ABC offered "Nightmare in Badham County," posing rather nervously as an exposé of women's prisons in the South. "Slavery is not a thing of the past!" screamed the ads. "The sadistic sheriff knows it. The psychotic warden knows it. But two girls learn it the hard way."
>
> So did the viewer, [said O'Connor, who went on to describe the show as] . . .two hours of relentless sado-masochistic titillation, overseen by tough women guards decked out in halter and high-

powered rifles. A young virgin, after being brought to the middle-aged warden for his perverted pleasures, committed suicide. Inmates were killed and secretly buried. Others were brutally beaten. Broad hints of lesbianism were added for good measure.[5]

"And prime-time TV," charged O'Connor, "chalked up still another milestone in its tireless effort to 'serve the public interest, convenience, and necessity.' "

This sort of glamorization of sexual perversity, plus the routine overabundance of rape and rapists on every TV crime show, has seriously distorted viewers' perception of rape and sex. Rape is used as an enticing attention-getter. It is eroticized, while the true horror and trauma of the victim is lost.

The result is that, according to Ann Kaye, community coordinator for the "Rape Project" of the County Crisis Center in Macomb County, Michigan "many men confuse rape with sex and feel that to be a man they must act like the movie hero-rapist." She even went so far as to warn that "until TV stops perpetuating the crime of rape by portraying a glamorized, eroticized, sexual view of rape, we will continue to see the number of rapes rise in this country."[6]

Dr. Bertram S. Brown, director of the National Institute of Mental Health, didn't go quite that far. But he agreed that "the blending of sex and violence as presented in some recent films perpetuates the confusion of both."[7] He went on to caution that when sex and violence are combined, the potentially harmful emotional impact could be multiplied. The following examples support his warning.

In the fall of 1976, one installment of the made-for-TV movie "The Moneychangers" portrayed a violent and vivid homosexual assault by a gang of inmates in a prison shower. "They stopped short of showing the actual penetration of the victim," reported one father who saw the show. "But the sexual abuse was clear enough for anyone to determine—regardless of age. My thirteen-year-old boy remained terrified for months that he might do something wrong and land in jail and suffer the horror of a similar attack."

Another example of the emotional impact television's treatment of violent sex can have on adult viewers was reported by a young married couple who watched a March, 1977, episode of "Dog and Cat."

This cop show, featuring a male-female investigative team, involved the pursuit of a rapist who preyed only on famous, powerful, or otherwise successful women. The visual treatment of the rape attempts was only typical of television's portrayal of such scenes. But the rapist recorded his assaults and after one of his rapes he sat at the desk in his office and replayed it. As the camera shifted from the spinning reels of the tape recorder to the smiling, satisfied face of the rapist, viewers were subjected to the shockingly recognizable sounds of a rape: the shriek of surprise, the pleas of terror, the cries of pain, the moans of anguish, and finally heavy breathing and silence.

"The horror of it made me so sick I had to run out of the room," said the wife, who was in her mid-twenties. "I stayed upset for hours. I already live with the awful possibility of rape every time I go out alone at night. I don't need, and I can't take, that kind of reminder to replay in my mind every time I step out into a dark shopping center parking lot."

Yet the show that so horrified this one viewer and perhaps reinforced the rape-fears of countless women viewers across the country provided enticing entertainment for millions of Americans that Saturday night. This is a poignant illustration of TV's undeniable appeal to prurient interests.

Unfortunately, the dramatic programs aren't the only purveyors of sex on the tube. Comedies are equally exploitative. In fact, their promotion of permissiveness and promiscuity may be an even bigger threat to viewers' moral standards than the dramatic treatment of immorality. Today's Christians tune in and learn to laugh at the sordid side of what God created to be one of his most beautifully sensitive gifts to mankind.

One young Christian offered a disturbing example. "My wife and I turned on the set last week and caught a new show called 'Three's Company' (March, 1977). The comedy involved a young fellow moving into an apartment with two single gals. When I realized the tone of the series, I started counting the sexually suggestive lines. The tally came to more than one per minute for the thirty-minute show."

"It had to be one of the most immorally suggestive programs I've ever seen," he admitted. "But even so, I laughed all the way through it. It was very funny."

That's the danger of the sex-laced sit-coms. Their humor is naturally disarming. And whether the sexual barb is the occasional jab at the nymphomania of Sue Ann Nivens on the generally wholesome "Mary Tyler Moore Show" or an unceasing bombardment of suggestive salvos on something like "Three's Company," the resulting damage is the same. Every laughable line with a sexual innuendo or a double entendre acts as one more chink in the armor of acceptability.

The issue isn't with any particularly offensive line or scene, or even with a specific comedy or drama. The real danger is the cumulative impact of show after show, night after night. When viewers turn on their sets to relax and be entertained, they lower their discerning defenses. So even if television's flood of secular attitudes toward sex doesn't sweep away their own sexual standards, it's hard to believe it doesn't erode some of their sensitivities and at least affect their tolerance and acceptance of lower standards in others.

In recent years, many Christian parents have become alarmed about growing attitudes of permissiveness and sagging sexual standards. Many have directed their concern and complaints at the quality of and amoral approach to sex education in the public schools. But in light of television's potential to influence and persuade viewers, the public education offered on the screen may be an even bigger threat to Christian standards of sexual values and behavior than what is being taught in school classrooms.

Respected behavioral authorities Albert Bandura and Richard Walters explain that because of the norms of privacy in the home, North American children are afforded little opportunity to observe sexual behavior—little chance to model their sexual behavior after their parents. So with no other observational model to draw on, they are forced to rely on what they can learn from the media.[8]

This means that as long as parents ignore immorality on the tube, television presents a dangerous threat to a young person's development of sexual attitudes and standards in line with biblical morality. Yet despite the danger, many Christian adults are unaware of the sexual picture television is presenting to children.

One Illinois church youth worker was among the blissfully ignorant a few years ago. He and his wife held weekly Bible studies for junior-high students in their home and noticed a favorite topic of conversation was "Happy Days," which was fairly new at the time. Thinking he ought to know something about a show with such a loyal, enthusiastic audience, he tuned in to an episode.

The story line featured "the Fonz," glorying in his reputation as a ladies' man. Fonzie's talk about a recent date was filled with sexual inferences, furthered by his claim of prowess at unfastening bras with one hand. His younger admirers, Richie and Pottsy, were duly impressed and inspired. After some instruction from "the master" and some practice on a spare bra commandeered for the training, Richie asked Fonzie's most recent companion for a date.

He began the encounter, with obvious nervousness, on the living-room couch of the home where the girl was babysitting. He anxiously proceeded to kiss her while awkwardly fumbling with the back of her sweater. The girl was insulted by Richie's presumption. He left frustrated and disillusioned by the realization that the Fonz's claims had been pure braggadocio. She just wasn't that kind of girl.

The "moral" of the story was that reputations can be easily and unjustly damaged. But the story's "amoral" lesson was that this sort of sexual experimentation was something to be accepted as normal and even laughable.

"It shocked me to realize that this was the sort of sexual modeling the junior-high-age kids I was working with were getting every week," said the youth worker.

Whether it is Henry Winkler playing a super-cool Fonz who can snap his fingers and have every girl panting after him, or whether it's Farrah Fawcett-Majors, whose strategy for investigative success is always to be slinky, sexy, and suggestive, today's television heroes present a powerful message for youngsters developing sexual attitudes, standards, and behavior. And that message proclaims to young viewers that sex is something to be snickered at, to be used to manipulate people, and to be indiscriminately engaged in for personal enjoyment.

The beauty of sex, the purpose for which God created it, the guidelines He set for its fullest enjoyment, and its powerful potential as the most intimately sensitive communication between a husband and a wife are never portrayed on TV.

In fact, "Romance appears to be principally a pre-marital phenomenon, or one experienced with someone else's husband or wife," wrote Harry J. Skornia, educator and broadcaster. "In fact, marriage appears to dampen romantic and love interests considerably. It is a social convention still endured, but with little glamor or enthusiasm."[9]

The situation has certainly worsened in the years since Professor Skornia made his observation. Viewers' sensitivities have been dulled on almost every sexual subject. Homosexuality has not only come out of the closet, it has entered our living rooms by way of comedies, dramas, and even documentaries that no longer consider it a sin or a sickness but a state of being to be accepted and lived with as naturally as one's race or sexual gender. Prostitutes now play heroines in TV movies and provide comedy relief on many sit-coms. Promiscuity, rape, and countless other perversions are presented routinely in the course of weekly entertainment. The compulsion to break the next taboo seems irresistible.

When one realizes how fast and far television has gone with its sordid portrayal of sex, one has to wonder, "What's left? Where can it possibly go from here?"

Perhaps a more crucial question for a concerned Christian parent to ask is, "What can I do to combat the damage TV has done and is doing to the sexual values and standards of society, of my family, and of myself?"

5
Telebucks: A View from the Bottom Line

Before Christians can decide on an effective strategy for dealing with the television issue, before they can react to the violence and sex on the set, they must examine another facet of the medium. No one can have a complete picture of the television industry or a full understanding of its effect on viewers without considering that TV's prime basis for existence is its source of financial support: advertising.

The American public is so accustomed to the concept of "free commercial" television that the "commercial" part is often forgotten. People hear so much about Nielsen ratings and audience shares that they forget the ultimate programming decisions depend on the sponsors, not the public. Viewers seldom realize the television industry's ultimate goal is not to produce a program for the public, but to provide a public for a product.

When it comes to providing an audience, television has more success than any other medium. The number of television sets is twice the daily circulation of newspapers in the United States.[1] Radio's local outreach can't compete with that of the national TV networks for exposure. Even movies don't begin to compare. For example, more people saw the theater box-office blockbuster "The Godfather" the first time it was shown on TV than in its record-breaking, 30-month run on the big screen.

Yet "The Godfather" wasn't anywhere near a television audience record; it is not even ranked in the top twenty television audiences in history. According to Nielsen figures, "Roots" holds the all-time record; the series pulled a total of approximately 500 million viewers over the eight nights it was on in January, 1977. Before "Roots," the movie "Gone With the Wind" held the record for drawing more than 75 million viewers each night of its two-night stand.

Of course, such gigantic crowds aren't at all unusual for big televised sports attractions. The record TV sports audience was for the seventh game of the 1975 World Series: almost 78 million fans tuned in. The 1977 Super Bowl XI came in a close second with somewhere around 75 million viewers.

Audiences like that make advertisers eager to shell out their money despite the astronomical cost. According to *Advertising Age*, "Twenty minutes of commercials within the 3½-hour Super Bowl XI broadcast were fully sold, NBC reported. Prices for minutes ranged up to $250,000."[2]

Total TV advertising revenues for 1976 (network and local) climbed to over $6 billion.[3] So obviously,

Telebucks: A View from the Bottom Line

television advertising is big business. Just how big was emphasized by the Screen Actor's Guild when it reported that commercial actors make more money ($84 million in 1975) than all the Screen Actor Guild members in movies and TV combined.[4]

But can all that money really be worth it? Does TV advertising pay off?

Evidently advertisers think so, because they keep increasing their investments. Many have reaped great rewards. *Advertising Age* reported that Jell-O Pudding nearly doubled its sales using Bill Cosby commercials. Bing Crosby and his family's plugs for Minute Maid increased sales for that breakfast beverage 25 percent in two years. A cartooned stork that delivers dills instead of babies took Vlasic to the top of the pickle pile.[5] And in just six years, Liquid Plumr skyrocketed from a regional brand to the number one slot in the national drain cleaner market with the help of its strong commercial campaign.[6]

These are the kinds of examples TV executives cite when they're trying to peddle some tube time to a prospective client. And these are the kinds of results the advertising clients dream of when they try to rationalize their whopping television advertising budgets. Neither the industry officials nor the clients seem to doubt that TV ads can make a difference; they just aren't sure of what or how much. Some campaigns may flop. But that's a gamble the advertisers are willing to take until actual results can be measured in gross sales and net profits.

But not all of TV's advertising effects may show up in the corporate ledger books. Many of television's staunchest critics question the impact on viewers who are subjected to commercial after commercial, appeal after appeal. Some TV opponents are as adamant in their attacks on what they see to be the evils of advertising as they are in blasting TV for its excessive violence.

Dr. Mark Shedd, the Department of Education commissioner for the state of Connecticut, pinpointed the primary center of critics' concern when he said, "We should be deeply disturbed by pressure-selling tactics directed at children, hawking a great variety of sugar-saturated products and junk food, among other things."[7] He went on to say he considered TV advertising a threat to the mental, dental, and physical health of America's young.

Dr. Shedd's concern, which is shared by many other parents and educators, is the way big business has zeroed in on children as an exploitable consumer target. Dr. Michael B. Rothenberg complained, "While the Code of Hammurabi in 2250 B.C. made selling something to a child or buying something from a child without power of attorney a crime punishable by death, in 1975 A.D. our children are exposed to some 350,000 television commercials by the time they reach 18."[8]

Opponents of child-aimed TV advertising favor Hammurabi's strategy. They question the morality of attempting to exploit children as consumers. They argue that children aren't experientially equipped to make the kind of consumer choices confronting them on the tube. They point out that children's decisions are too often based on what they want and what looks good, not on what they need. And this undeniable susceptibility of children is a good argument for protecting them from the promotional gimmickery that so often marks TV commercials.

Defenders of the present advertising setup contend, however, that a youngster's early experience with advertising may be beneficial and perhaps even necessary for an adequate development of important consumer skills. They insist children's ads help prepare them for the pressures and decisions they someday will have to face in the adult world.

But even granting this possible value—and few critics do—child-aimed commercials deserve concern. *Newsweek* reported that of the more than $400 million worth of the "kid-vid" commercials aired in 1976, "more than 70 percent of the ads . . . peddle sugar-coated cereals, candy, and chewing gum. Laced with action-packed attention grabbers and pitched by an ingratiating adult authority figure, such messages hook children on poor eating habits before they develop the mental defenses to resist."[9]

Yet, while television advertising is criticized as a threat that will turn today's children into a generation of overweight super-consumers, the potential dangers may not stop there. In a recent investigation into the attitudinal response of children to TV commercials, Dr. Thomas Bever, a Columbia University psychologist, and Martin Smith, an advertising executive, turned up some thought-provoking findings.

Bever and Smith discovered that youngsters between five and six years old unquestioningly accepted the claims of TV ads. Seven- to ten-year-olds showed a growing tension and anger toward their own inability to cope with misleading advertising. This indicated they were learning from experience that everything TV said didn't seem to be true, but they didn't know who to blame. By the time they were ten, they came to realize advertising was an institutionally accepted hypocrisy and became cynical of all advertising. And by the age of eleven or twelve, the children in the study seemed to consider societal hypocrisy as an acceptable fact of life. [10]

Bever and Smith concluded, "TV advertising is stimulating pre-adolescent children to think about socially accepted hypocrisy. They may be too young to cope with such thoughts without permanently distorting their views of morality, society, and business." [11]

A certain wariness may be a valuable trait in this age of commercialism and consumerism. But if the underlying attitude of skepticism taught by TV commercials carries over to other institutions or to relationships with people and society as a whole, then Christian parents need to be concerned. Television advertising may be acting as a catalyst of bitter experience—hardening youngsters into caustic, cautious cynics by the time they become teen-agers. The commercials may be creating a barrier of defensive distrust that hampers any honest, open, accepting relationship with others, with the church, or with God.

Adults, too, may be victimized rather than benefited by the kind of advertising they are exposed to on the television screen. Even a healthy dose of objective adult caution may not provide protection enough, for while some ads are straightforward product pitches, others are extremely deceptive.

One commercial for a leading pain reliever offers a perfect example. A famous TV actor who once played a doctor on a long-running series comes on the screen and speaks with a tone of sincerity and care. He says, "If I told you this pain reliever worked better than regular aspirin, you might not buy it. But would you listen if there was medical evidence? In two medical research studies on pain other than headache, at a large hospital and a leading university, doctors reported that this brand worked significantly better than the regular aspirin tablet. Right. Doctors reported that this brand has worked better than aspirin. So next time you get a headache, try it."

Where's the manipulation? It's much easier to spot in the black and white of the printed page than it is when the nice man in the ad is speaking so kindly and warmly. Carefully buried back in the middle of the commercial, the medical studies were *for pain other than headache*. But by the end of the commercial the pitch is *So the next time you get a headache, try it*.

Unfortunately, such deception is not only acceptable to the people who make TV ads, they consider it inevitable. The chairman of a leading advertising agency revealed, "It's almost impossible to make a comparative 30-second TV commercial whose fairness, truthfulness, and capacity to mislead is beyond challenge." Truth, he said, is "so precariously balanced that she may be attended by a bodyguard of lies."[12]

He was talking specifically about comparative commercials, where one product is compared against another. But that attitude toward truthfulness in any commercial ought to arouse the ire of any viewer.

The real effectiveness of television commercials, however, lies not in deceptive or tricky wordings designed to mislead or sneak past a thoughtful viewer. Their real power rests in their subtle persuasive ability to implant a sentence, a thought, or a word in the subconscious mind.

Many people turn away from the set to talk, to get refreshments, or to do something else when a commercial comes on. Some viewers even make a conscious effort to think about something else, to direct their attention elsewhere when an ad appears on the screen. And some who do watch the commercials insist that "I watch, but I don't think the ads really have any effect on me. When a show's over, I can't even remember who sponsored it."

But those viewers who can't recall a single sponsor's name after an evening of television entertainment, those who consciously "tune out" commercials, and even those who went to a refrigerator within earshot of the set may still be significantly affected by commercials they don't remember hearing or seeing.

"The function of advertising," as explained by an expert in designing commercials, Tony Schwartz, "is to give the consumer materials and associations that will be evoked by the stimulus of seeing the product. . . . Those of us who create commercials are in the business of structuring recall."[13]

So it doesn't matter whether or not a viewer thinks long and hard about what mouthwash sponsors his favorite prime-time show. The real test of the ad's effectiveness comes when he spots the familiar-shaped bottle of green liquid on the drugstore shelf and recalls a positive feeling. He may even remember, "Yeah, this is the stuff that doesn't taste mediciney." If that happens, the commercial worked.

One teen-ager who worked for one of the big fast-food chains testified to the recall effectiveness of one series of musical commercials. He came home from his job one day to complain, "If I hear one more customer singing 'Have it your way' I think I'll go crazy!" He's just lucky he didn't work for the competition where every other customer might subject him to an order of two-all-beef-patties-special-sauce-lettuce-cheese-pickles-onions-on-a-sesame-seed-bun.

The impact of such familiar advertising jingles and chants is powerfully pervasive. The potential for a commercial message to infiltrate the mind against a viewer's will was demonstrated by one young woman who classified herself as a militant teetotaler. "The tunes on some of the beer commercials are so catchy," she said. "Sometimes I'll be driving somewhere, or even sitting at my desk at work, and I'll catch myself humming one of the beer commercial choruses. I can't seem to help it, even though I have very strong feelings against drinking and against the ads."

In some ways, the subliminal implanting of a message or a song in the subconscious is as much a testimony to the miraculous capacity of the human mind as it is evidence of the insidious power of any particular commercial. But the makers of those ads recognize and play on that capability.

In fact, as viewers grow more and more

accustomed to the electric images on the screen, they are being conditioned to absorb commercial messages at a faster rate. The ad-makers realize it and plan to take advantage of the new viewer skill. The J. Walter Thompson Co., a leading advertising agency, now predicts that in the near future, standard TV spots will be a rapid-fire three seconds long.

"A typical three-second spot for Monroe shock absorbers in 1992 might show in quick succession: a toy car jumping fitfully, entering a Monroe shock absorber container and emerging from the other side rolling smoothly. In three seconds, the message is clear: Monroe shock absorbers give a smooth ride."[14]

But by 1992 even the three-second spots may be too slow. The Thompson agency thinks that by then one-second flashes will be long enough to transmit a message that can be easily comprehended by a TV-conditioned viewer.

Christians worried about the TV issue and about television's threat to viewers need to be wary of its easily assimilated messages that can clutter the subconscious and perhaps affect thinking and decisions that ought to be clearly and solely based on Christian principles. Christians ought to be incensed at any obvious or intentional deception. And certainly Christian parents need to recognize the effect of television advertising on children. But from a Christian perspective, the most ominous portent of TV commercials is their appeal to deeply felt human needs with their false promise of hope and solution.

Vance Packard understood this twenty years ago

when he wrote *The Hidden Persuaders*. He explained that advertisements weren't just selling a product, they were marketing answers for hidden human needs. He catalogued a number of those needs, including a reassurance of worth, ego gratification, and a sense of power.[15]

The format and some of the products may have changed since Packard made his analysis. But today's TV ads aim at those same basic human needs. A commercial that tells a viewer "you deserve a break today" reassures him of his worth as a person while at the same time reminding him that if his financial worth isn't so high, he can still get a good meal for under a dollar. The ad that comments "you never looked so good" is definitely an attempt to gratify the ego, even if it is trying to sell cosmetics to make viewers look even better. And the airline proclamation that "You're the Boss" is designed to evoke a sense of power in the potential customer.

Hardly any felt need or human problem escapes the attention or use of some television commercial. In search of marital bliss? If trouble is brewing, Mrs. Olson's coffee is guaranteed to perk up the marriage. After one cup of her terrific brand, both husband and wife are happy and smiling again. Another boon for husband-wife relations seems to be Geritol. Every husband on those commercials expresses his warm, smiling pride and love for his wife because "she takes Geritol every day."

Another overused commercial angle is the appeal to sexual desires. Many ads attract attention with suggestive and sexual overtones. Others openly promise an end to sexual problems—like the toothpaste spot that begins with, "How's your love life?"

Is life dull and boring? Have you lost all your zest and vitality? Any one of the colas offers hope. "Join the Pepsi generation" for fun and excitement. "Coke adds life," too. Or viewers can just follow the carefree example of any one of the exciting characters who sings about "Me and my RC."

Concerned about the needs and security of your family? Who isn't? That is why commercials for everything from soup to life insurance promise to feed the nutritional or financial "needs" of your family.

Commercials promise a satisfying solution for any and every imaginable human problem, from heartburn to social ostracism. The ads sell salvation for any predicament, with a new commercial gospel promising love, happiness, success, security, personal fulfillment, and the satisfaction of any other human need or desire.

The danger is in the gospel of materialism, which promises solutions by spending more money. The TV can flash on a new automobile, proclaim the status and acceptance that go with it, and even mature Christians will find it hard to resist dropping by the dealer for a firsthand look. The message of materialism, flashed through the tube in the image of cars, homes, vacations, or whatever, may become a subconscious urge of devastating power.

One Christian couple in their twenties admitted that they ran up $18,000 on their credit cards in four months. "It all looked so good and so much in reach," the wife confessed as they sold their house and their personal items to try to stave off their creditors.

The materialistic theology on the set can lead to that trap. Christians, of all viewers, ought to realize that the appeal of television advertising is in direct contrast to the biblical gospel they believe in. God's gospel says "deny yourself," "die to self." The gospel of materialism says "indulge yourself," "live it up." Jesus' instruction to "seek ye first the kingdom of God" is too often lost in the glittering picture projected on the screen. Christians too can be duped into chasing after TV's materialistic mirage.

The basic tenet of this new materialistic gospel is self-indulgence. But the appeal to self is hardly a new strategy—it's the oldest temptation in the book. Satan himself easily could have built his first advertising campaign for apples around the slogan, "Try it, you'll like it!"

Today's television commercials have just embellished and glamorized the old appeal. The result, according to Roy Truby, superintendent of public instruction in Idaho, is a new theology.

> There is what we might call a "theology of television" developing as a prevailing influence on American society. The ads constantly tell us to seek greater pleasure through more consumption.
>
> One beer ad, for example, says, "You only go around once in life, so you have to grab all the gusto you can get." This kind of philosophy may lead only to frustration and disappointment. Philosophers through the years, since Aristotle, have rejected this

theology as a way of life. But somehow the ads make us feel that to have nothing less than too much is un-American.[16]

That effect is intentional. "One of the main jobs of the advertiser," said Ernest Dichter, president of the Institute of Motivational Research, "is not so much to sell the product as to give moral permission to have fun without guilt."[17]

Yet at the same time the gospel of materialism is attempting to allay all guilt about selfish indulgence, it also tries to divert attention and concern by creating new false guilts and anxieties. Ring around the collar, bitter coffee, and dingy yellow kitchen floors become cardinal sins. Water-spotted crystal, baggy pantyhose, and the threat of embarrassing foot odor become serious anxiety-producing concerns. The danger for viewers, especially Christian viewers who have the real Truth and the real Answer, is that concern and attention can be channeled away from the most pressing human needs and problems.

So TV advertising presents a dual threat to Christian viewers. If its promotional propaganda doesn't attract them to an acceptance of the false values of materialism, it may convince them to actually care whether or not they can see their reflections in their everyday china. And that may be worse.

In either case, the world's most important message—God's gospel—may go unnoticed and unheard. The most spectacular offer of all time may be lost in the commercial clutter that offers nothing but a video flim-flam of vain words and hollow promises.

6
The Perils of
Cause and Effect

While the evidence continues to mount against television's content and its insidious impact on viewers, few of the people who are even aware of the findings have made any personal application by rethinking or changing their own families' viewing habits. Even those who readily condemn the surplus of sex and violence for its potential harmful effect on children and on others who are "more susceptible" often discount the chance of being affected themselves.

"We can keep it all in perspective," they say. "We know what's real and what isn't!"

But anyone that confident of immunity from television's effects probably doesn't realize the most crucial implication of the television medium—the basic reason television's content can pose a threat to any viewer. They don't understand that by its very living and moving nature, by its total saturation of society, television purports to reflect reality—to BE reality.

TV's sex, its violence, its blatant materialism, and all its other secular values combine to make one powerful piece of propaganda. Its message pounds continuously into the viewer's subconscious mind, asserting with the authority of a thousand Walter Cronkites, "That's the way it is. That's the way it really is." The more the viewer is exposed, the more pervasive the message. Gradually, biblical truth begins to blur into secular falsehoods as that fine line between everyday fact and television fiction fades and disappears.

When children fail to integrate common television fantasies into the reality of everyday life, the consequences can be tragic. For example:

On October 16, 1949, fifteen-year-old Richard Elliott and his ten-year-old brother Robert were left at home to watch television while their parents went out for dinner in nearby Los Angeles. It was Sunday night and the boys were watching a Hopalong Cassidy movie.

As gunfighting erupted on the screen, Richard went to his room to get a gun to show his little brother the "kind of gun they use in the West." He was playing with the .32 caliber weapon when it went off.

The shot struck Robert in the head. He fell and lay writhing and moaning on the floor. Then, "testifying that he was unable to see him suffer so, Richard backed up, and with mixed feelings of mercy and cowboy courage, fired a second shot into the head of his brother. The little one died of his wounds. His pains were over."[1]

On August 25, 1966, the *New York Times* printed the following report:

Television chiefs issued a warning to millions of youngsters today after an inquest on a boy who died while imitating his masked and cloaked hero, "Batman." . . . His father . . . told the inquest yesterday he thought his son, hanged while wearing a homemade Batman-style outfit, had been leaping from a cabinet in the garden shed when his neck caught in a nylon loop hanging from the roof. The inquest verdict was misadventure. After the inquest the father said that he hoped the Batman show would be taken off British television. "It is far too dramatic and hair-raising," he said. "It encourages children to attempt the impossible."

A television spokesman said, "We regret that the death of Charles Lee should be attributed to his viewing of Batman. Young viewers are cautioned that they should make no attempt to imitate Batman's activities. Before each episode young viewers are reminded that Batman does not in fact fly and that all of his exploits are accomplished by means of his secret equipment."[2]

These are but two bits of evidence that show how children's perception and real-life reactions can be blurred or distorted by the false picture of life presented on the TV screen. But kids aren't the only victims of deception. Adults also have trouble telling truth from TV fiction.

For example, "In a courtroom incident related to us by a lawyer, the counsel for the defense leapt to his feet, objecting, 'Your Honor, the prosecutor is badgering the witness!' The judge replied that he, too, had seen that objection raised on the Perry Mason show, but unfortunately, it was not included in the California code."[3]

As further evidence, consider the public response to the television show, "Marcus Welby, M.D." In the first five years that show was on the air, it drew 250,000 letters from viewers. Most of those letters contained requests for medical advice.[4]

Writing to fictional TV doctors for suggested treatment may seem naive, even humorous. But the implications aren't funny at all. That kind of response is just one more indication of what is possibly the single most significant and threatening problem television presents for viewers—its distortion of reality.

E. B. White predicted such a dilemma after seeing a TV demonstration back in 1938. He wrote, "A door closing, heard over the air, a face contorted, seen in a panel of light, these will emerge as the real and the true. And when we bang on the door of our own cell or look into another's face, the impression will be of mere artifice."[5]

That prediction, which probably sounded like the wildest science fiction in 1938, is coming true today. Television's picture of reality is readily accepted by great numbers of viewers.

The 1975 Gerbner Report, the annual survey of violent content in television programming, found that people who watch a lot of TV "see the real world as more dangerous and frightening than those who watch very little. Heavy viewers are less trustful of their fellow citizens and more fearful of the real world."[6]

Gerbner also discovered that people who got a heavy dose of the disproportionate number of law enforcement and white-collar workers on TV overestimate their number in real life. In other words, viewers used television action as their gauge of reality.

The implications for Christians are alarming! If TV content can distort our view of something as concrete as the demographic makeup of society, what subtle effects might it have on something as abstract as Christian attitudes and values? How might it warp the attitudes and views of Christian children and young people? If Christians subconsciously and unquestioningly accept what they see on TV as an accurate benchmark of the reality around them, how many decisions might be influenced by false perceptions? Christians might well be walking in the wrong light—the distorted light of the blue-grey screen in the living room—not the Light and Truth of Christ and His revelation in God's Word.

So far, television violence and its effects have drawn more attention and study than any other characteristic of the medium. Gerbner's findings on people's perceptions of violence aroused much interest and concern. But other distortions should be just as alarming for Christians.

What, for example, does TV teach about sexual realities?

TELEGARBAGE

Television's preoccupation with sex, its promotion of permissiveness, has already been discussed. But Keith Davis, a researcher and contributor to the "Report of the Commission on Obscenity and Pornography" (1970), underlined the implications. He disagreed with the commission's "no harm" conclusion and said, "It is hard to imagine that what a society tolerates in its mass media as a portrayal of sexual reality will not come to be the kind of sexual reality that society's next generation lives."[7]

Deep down, some viewers may know the promise of the picture won't translate into real life. But the overwhelming evidence acted out on the screen is convincing, and so the tube is seldom questioned.

In some ways TV's high credibility has been earned. Every television program has its own stage designers, prop men, and technical advisers to insure realism in every shot and every set."Adam-12," the long-running and rerunning cop show, was an ideal example of the industry's devotion to detail. The police procedures portrayed on that show were so accurate that, according to Martin Milner, co-star of the series, some small-town law enforcement departments requested copies of certain episodes to use as inexpensive training films for their officers.

One benefit resulting from all the care and concern for realism has been the wealth of incidental education television provides viewers. Most Americans can readily recognize and even describe the appearance and many of the procedures of a hospital operating room. The average ten-year-old can explain in detail how criminals are arrested, booked, jailed, and tried. The sights and sounds of corporate board rooms, ocean-liner decks, movie studios, even maximum-security prisons are familiar to millions of people who have experienced none of them.

But the factual background accuracy that teaches so many so much about places and practices they might never see can also contribute to the blurring of the act and the actual in the subconscious mind of the viewer.

Bruce Baker, police chief of Portland, Oregon, told of a group of fourth-graders who had recently visited his office during a departmental tour. "Their questions," he said, "were primarily centered around whether we had undercover cars with mag wheels like Starsky and Hutch, and whether it hurt when policemen got shot as often as they did on various police programs. (The latter was accompanied by oral simulations of gunfire and clutching of breasts in mortal agony.) Almost all their interest focused upon the rare extremes of law enforcement involving violent encounters with guns."[8]

Whether the case involves fourth-graders looking for undercover cars with mag wheels or thousands of adults seeking Marcus Welby's professional diagnosis, the symptoms are the same. The fine details of televised action can convincingly blur the factual and the fictional.

Another dangerous distorting factor of television is its leveling effect; it reduces everything shown on the screen to the same level of reality or unreality. The prime-time movie about a terrorist plot makes the 11:00 news clips of the latest Northern Ireland bombings seem like an instant replay. Both provide entertainment to be viewed with equal involvement or detachment.

Howard Cosell analyzes a play on Monday night football with as much intensity and seriousness as John Chancellor and David Brinkley exhibit in a discussion of the President's State of the Union message. War, politics, game shows, sports, and beauty pageants are all presented with a sense of equal importance. Everything is entertainment—with the accompanying ads, previews, and announcers whose job is to keep it all interesting. The goal is always to keep the viewers from switching channels in search of more drama and excitement.

TV also distorts reality by presenting a simplistic picture of life. In the real world, personalities are terribly complex, motives are mixed, and some problems go unsolved forever. But television projects a world of clarity and simplicity. People demonstrate clear-cut dominant characteristics, motives are obviously plain (if they're not, the star of the show always explains them during the epilogue), and unless the plot is to be continued next week, every show ends with all problems resolved.

The distortion of simplicity is magnified by TV's compression of life into the immediacy of the present. Plot after plot, based on potentially life-shattering conflicts, is concluded in a single thirty- to ninety-minute show. TV life races from crisis to crisis, from excitement to more excitement. Time is compressed by omitting the mundane and the ordinary. TV ignores the routine to concentrate on the action of life.

It's no wonder then, as Marshall McLuhan said, that "the TV child cannot see ahead because he wants more involvement, and he cannot accept a fragmentary and merely visualized goal or destiny in learning or in life."[9]

How much does this kind of attitude toward reality affect basic values? How much has television's emphasis on excitement influenced our society's growing sense of dissatisfaction with life? How much has today's epidemic of depression and despair over the complex problems of life been compounded by television's distorted presentation of life as simple and certain?

Any attempt to answer these questions specifically would be pure speculation. But it seems certain from the research data and from observation that people's actions, attitudes, and even values are shaped, at least in part, by their perception of televised "reality."

Gerbner and Gross see it all as part of the historical pattern. They wrote, "All societies have evolved ways of explaining the world to themselves and their children. Socially constructed 'reality' gives a coherent picture of what exists, what is important, what is related to what, and what is right."[10]

In the past, this was a function of literature, families, and interpersonal training at home or church. But in modern America, television has taken over this teaching role. Today's "socially constructed reality" is decided by some unseen programmer in the network hierarchy. Then that "reality" is performed in two-dimensional patterns of flashing dots and lines of light on a little box that sits in the corner of some room in almost every house.

Joe Bayly wrote that in approaching 1984, the danger "is not Big Brother observing human life in every room by TV cameras who thereby controls life; Big Brother performs on TV in every room and thereby determines life."[11]

What has made this new determiner of reality so deceptive is that the very importance it has gained in society and the prominence it plays in everyday life makes it seem like the only teller of truth. Unless something appears on TV, it is generally perceived as inconclusive, unimportant, or nonexistent. For many members of American society, television is the sole source of "public knowledge."

Yet there are gaping holes in the portrait of reality on exhibit on TV. The ordinariness of living is left out and glazed over with glamor. The positive normality and health that marks many real families is seldom mirrored by the medium. And when is spiritual reality ever portrayed on the screen? What picture of God is presented, apart from the occasional Billy Graham specials?

If, as Gerbner and Gross contend, "Representation in the fictional world signifies social existence" and "absence means symbolic annihilation,"[12] then much of what Christians hold as crucial and good is being lost on today's society. It is being lost because our most powerful medium is presenting an incomplete and distorted picture of life.

The Christian who wants a clear perception of

reality, the Christian who seeks to shape his values around a biblical world view, the Christian who wants the rest of the world to see and understand the reality he lives by, the Christian who wants his children to realize the reality of Christ and to follow a Christian lifestyle faces a tough problem. He must recognize the importance and influence of television. And he must search for some viable solutions for society, for his family, and for himself.

7
Tele-addiction:
"God Help the Children"

An enormous stockpile of studies and evidence suggests that television's distorted dependence on sexual and violent content, its clouding of reality, and its commercial plugs for materialism can affect viewers of all ages. But TV's impact certainly isn't limited to those most studied areas.

The totality of television, the almost exalted position it has attained in society, makes the medium a potential shaping and changing force in every aspect of American life. Some of its effects on viewers are obvious. Many are subtle.

Since children seem to be the most susceptible viewers—studies show they react more intensely to television than adults—Christian parents need to be aware and concerned about TV's impact on their children. That impact involves much more than most parents seem to realize.

Few adults have noticed the extent to which

television has so completely changed childhood just in the area of time. Children of past generations spent much of their time playing games, experimenting on curiosities, and exploring the world around them. But children of today spend their time with their eyes glued to the television set and their bottoms firmly planted on the living-room rug.

Nearly half of the twelve-year-olds studied by Dr. Gerbner watched an almost unbelievable average of six or more hours a day. Thirty years ago parents would never have conceived of, let alone permitted, their children devoting that much time to any one activity. Yet many parents today actually encourage their children to watch TV. They do it without a second thought—often for no better reason than to keep them occupied and out of Mommy's and Daddy's hair.

Television plays such an important part in the daily life and schedule of the average American child that many families have to organize everything else around it. Supper and shopping trips must be planned around reruns of "Batman" and "Hogan's Heroes." Saturday mornings are the sacred domain of "Spiderman" and countless other cartoon favorites; any special family activity must wait until afternoon. And of course, any prime-time program can become a weapon or a bargaining point in the battle of the bedtime blues.

While the amount of time television takes from childhood is fairly obvious, an even more critical effect may not be. Too much tube time can distort children's relationships with others.

Tele-addiction: "God Help the Children"

Television can isolate children from the interpersonal interaction necessary for their healthy growth and maturity. The time spent studying life on the screen is stolen from other activities of relationship—playing, communicating, and learning from others. Dr. David Pearl of the National Institute of Mental Health suspects TV "has displaced many of the normal interactional processes between parents and children. . . . Those kinds of interactions are essential for maximum development."[1]

An overload of television's electric people can even short-circuit a youngster's capability for real-life relationships. According to eminent child psychologist Bruno Bettelheim, "Children who have been taught or conditioned to listen passively most of the day to the warm verbal communication coming from the TV screen, the deep emotional appeal of the so-called TV personality, are often unable to respond to real persons because they arouse so much less feeling than the skilled actor."[2]

Children need adult contact. They need relationships for reassurance and instruction in the ways of adult society. So in the rush and confusion of modern society, with its busy parents and broken homes, with the near-extinction of the extended family, TV has taken up the slack. It offers answers and insights for many children who are desperately searching for an understanding of the adult world.

The picture of life presented on television, however, is far from reassuring. Television adults are constantly causing trouble or are in trouble. They are often cruel, dishonest, immoral, and unpredictable.

Many are confused and unsure of themselves. So the insecure child who is looking for clues to living and surviving in the grown-up world may see a terrible, disillusioning picture on TV.

One reason is that TV prematurely forces children to acquire an adult outlook on life—to grow up too fast. They have to, in order to understand the adult world presented on the screen. They have to, in order to follow and enjoy television's adult-centered entertainment.

During the early seventies, when "All In the Family" was the most popular show on the air, this very adult comedy drew the largest child audience of any regular television show. The Nielsen ratings showed that nine million children under the age of twelve watched Archie Bunker and his family each week. Research on the impact of that show on children revealed that many of them weren't getting the same meaning and message from the show as their parents who watched with them. But those young viewers were actively striving to learn, understand, and appreciate the adult insights, attitudes, and actions on the screen.[3]

The resulting implications of this kind of adult exposure to life can't be measured. But by the time most kids are ten or twelve, they've seen it all. They know the adult world in and out—at least they know the adult world as it is portrayed on the screen. They've developed the insights and the attitudes needed for understanding that picture. They've seen everything from the wonderful miracle of birth to the gruesome horror of war in vivid living and dying color right in their living rooms, and they're no longer curious, easily impressed children. They are experienced, knowledgeable, and often cynical adults.

The natural result of this overdose of television has been a severe case of mass addiction for adults as well as for children. The cumulative input of hour after hour, day after day, year after year, electronic stimulation finally takes its toll. Some viewers come to depend on it as a mind wash, an escape from the complicated reality of everyday life. Others crave the arousal, the pick-up they get from the simulated action.

Viewing becomes a ritual. It doesn't really matter what is shown; the addicted viewer will watch anyway. The television industry acknowledges this with its widespread explanation known in the business as the "Theory of the Least Objectionable Program." This LOP theory holds that viewers are going to have to watch something. If nothing good is on, the majority of people will tune in to the show they consider the least objectionable. The goal for the networks then isn't necessarily to provide quality; it is to present something less objectionable than the competition—to feed the viewers' habits without offending them.

Further proof of television's addictive nature is the occurrence in many viewers of withdrawal symptoms when viewing is reduced. Parents of children who participated in a study sponsored by *Redbook* magazine found that when television was restricted, their children reacted with increased fits of temper. They acted "moodier than usual, sitting and staring at the ground," they became more irritable, and one youngster even took out his hostility by turning rough and mean with the family pets.[4]

When the Society for Rational Psychology in Germany paid volunteers to abstain from television for a year, they discovered that adults also suffer withdrawal. Not one of the 184 paid volunteers lasted longer than five months. "Tension and quarrelling increased, even wife-beating reached a new intensity, and the volunteers' love life took a nose dive. With the sets restored, the symptoms disappeared."[5]

Not surprisingly, the cumulative effect of the TV habit works much like a drug. Gradually it narcoticizes viewers into passivity. Children who should be out getting bruised, dirty, and generally exhausted, exercise only their blinking eyelids as they sit entranced for hours in front of the tube.

Adults too are in danger of atrophy. While one of America's most critical medical problems is overweight people, millions of men limit their exercise to an occasional twist in an easy chair as they try to lend a little body English to their favorite quarterback on autumn weekend afternoons.

For many, the stagnation may be mental as well as physical. How much has the habit of reading suffered because it takes less effort to flick on the set for the evening than it does to enjoy a good book? Millions of devoted fans stay up every night to watch Johnny Carson make casual and often inane conversation with a long list of celebrities; how many of those viewers ever attempt to engage their families or friends in meaningful discussions the next day?

The point is obvious: for many viewers—children and adults—life has become a spectator sport. It's much easier to watch it parade by on the screen than it is to get in step and become actively involved.

As a disconcerting side effect, television addiction may shackle creativity.

A University of Southern California research team exposed 250 elementary students—who had been judged mentally gifted—to three weeks of intensive viewing. Tests conducted before and after the experiment found a marked drop in all forms of creative ability except verbal skill. Some teachers are encountering children who cannot understand a simple story without visual illustrations. "TV has taken away the child's ability to form pictures in his mind," says child-development expert Dorothy Cohen at New York City's Bank Street College of Education.[6]

Many teachers and educators have noticed and reported that children's free play, which has always been marked by a high degree of spontaneity and imagination, is often structured closely after TV programs. Certainly a lot of childlike creativity survives, but instead of fresh, exciting, newly conjured-up characters, more and more imagined identities fit the standardized pattern of a TV hero. It seems every preschooler in the country wants to play the Bionic Woman or the Six-Million-Dollar Man.

But perhaps a bigger problem than its harmful

effects on creativity, its addictive nature, and its reinforcement of passivity, is the variety of questionable values television shows, legitimizes, and teaches. Some of the most pervasive have been mentioned in the chapters on violence, sex, and advertising. But there are more. And these too should be of crucial concern for Christian parents.

One of television's most devastating dangers is its obvious and constant promotion of alcohol. A fairly recent study of 249 television shows conducted by the *Christian Science Monitor* claimed that alcoholic drinks played a part in eight of ten prime-time programs. Booze is a popular prop for too many programs, as *Chicago Tribune* TV reviewer, Marilynn Preston, pointed out.

> On "Switch" a tumbler of Scotch becomes a permanent extension of Robert Wagner's arm. Sweet Lou Grant keeps a bottle in his bottom desk drawer. Maude likes to come home to a double-anything and make it fast. And Archie isn't Archie until Edith trots in with that first beer of the night.
>
> So what? So people drink liquor on TV; so what else is new? So plenty of people in the country drink—about 100 million, according to statistics—so big, bubbling deal? So a lot of people are concerned, because of those 100 million, at least 10 million are confirmed alcoholics, and that is a big deal. Because the estimated annual economic loss to the country from alcohol abuse is a very sobering $25 billion. Because more teens than ever are wrecking their livers and maybe their lives as alcohol use, and abuse, hits record highs among adolescents.[7]

Tele-addiction: "God Help the Children"

The television industry claims concern. And it does offer occasional public service announcements aimed at the drinking problem. Yet the broadcasting industry allows itself to be used as an advertising vehicle. The liquor industry pays for commercials and celebrities to convince viewers to imbibe. Talented and glamorous stars like Burt Bacharach and Angie Dickinson sell it with song and sex. Athletes like Mickey Mantle and Whitey Ford coax viewers with boasts of belonging to "The Beer-Drinker's Hall of Fame."

The most powerful pitches for drinking, however, aren't even paid for by the liquor industry—they're provided free by the programs. This programmed propaganda may be more low-key than the commercials, but the arguments are no less convincing. "Everybody drinks; there's no harm in it. . . . Drinks help the good times roll. . . . Booze relaxes. . . . Drunk is sometimes funny, often excusable. . . . Drinking is sophisticated, expected. . . . It's a big part of glamorous, excitement-packed lives."

The message is unmistakable. And while the television influence on growing alcohol abuse in America is more debatable than measurable, the value TV places on drinking can't possibly be helping to solve what has become a serious and terribly complicated social problem.

Human behavior itself is a terribly complicated phenomenon. Exact causes can't be precisely pinpointed. But a Minnesota criminal judge, Doyle Aultman, pointed out that if "the 'hard-sell' [advertising] is causing behavioral change reflected in purchases and profits which we can readily measure, then there is good reason to believe the 'soft-sell' [program concepts] is causing similar behavioral change—but it deals with attitudes which are much more difficult to measure."[8]

Judge Aultman's testimony primarily concerned the issue of violence. But since evidence indicates that what he said is true of violence, sex, and reality, TV's promotion of alcohol and its more subtle promotion of a number of other values poses a real threat to viewers.

One of those other values is the attractiveness of affluence. Advertising promotes a gospel of materialism, but it doesn't stop when the commercial concludes. Many TV shows exhibit the trappings of affluence. The message is transmitted in the cars, the clothes, the homes, the furniture, and even in the food. (How often does any TV character stop at McDonald's for a bite to eat? Or even a steak house?)

As a result of TV's wonderland of wealth, Dr. Ernest G. Beier, a University of Utah psychologist, believes viewers learn from the dramas, the ads, and especially the game shows that affluence is not only desirable, but it may be had for the asking. Beier points out, "Most of the people watching, however, are not affluent, so that what is drummed into their heads is the message that they are in fact denied the 'good life' to which they are rightfully entitled."[9]

As a result, many children and adults base their wants and their material expectations on the standard of living and its symbols they see on the screen. For most of them, it's a tempting but unrealistic goal that can't help but create and foster bitterness or discontent.

Another attitude TV promotes is the importance of success—secular success. Affluence is often part of it. But success on TV also often means fame, power, glamorous friends, and good looks. If viewers compare what they see with what they are (and a number of studies show they do), their own personal shortcomings become glaringly obvious. So even viewers' self-images may be damaged or altered in response to TV's "success ethic."

Other attitudes, which should be just as disconcerting for Christians, are often woven inconspicuously into the fictional fabric of TV programming. A favorite philosophy of many of the corner-cutting cops is the old argument that the end justifies the means. TV usually ignores the term "sin." Wrong is defined as something that hurts another person; anything else is okay. Guilt, as seen on TV, is something you go to a psychiatrist to get rid of. And any meaningful belief in God is limited to little children, old ladies, and perhaps an earlier period in history—like "The Waltons" or "Little House on the Prairie." Occasional exceptions do exist, but unChristian and anti-Christian attitudes are more often the rule in television entertainment. What makes it all the more frightening is to realize that in today's confused and rapidly changing world, many people who want and need clear moral norms are searching the television screen for cues. It's true. Research done in Scandinavia found that many children say they watch TV "because it tells me what is right and wrong."[10]

What is just as alarming is that many adults also look to television for answers. Dr. Joseph Plummer, a social researcher for the Leo Burnett Advertising Agency, recently said in a lecture at Wheaton College Graduate School that his research shows millions of people watch television soap operas in attempts to solve problems in their own personal lives.

In some ways this influence is only natural. As regular daily or weekly guests in the home, TV characters are often better known and liked by viewers than most real-life friends and acquaintances. As an important part of viewers' peer groups, it is to be expected that these electronic friends, these hero-peers, can wield a powerful influence on the thinking and actions of viewers.

The problem dismays many Christian parents who feel helpless to control the impact of the electric input on their children. They know they don't like what they see, but they feel hopelessly inadequate to stop it. They are painfully aware that Marshall McLuhan's assessment was true when he wrote, "The family circle has widened. The worldpool of information fathered by electronic media . . . far surpasses any possible influence mom and dad can now bring to bear. Character is no longer shaped by only two earnest, fumbling experts. Now the whole world's a sage."[11]

But at the same time, the world's traditional values and structures are crumbling. New standards are being erected only to be toppled tomorrow by the next popular philosophy.

Christians attempting to stand their ground against the movements and the madness of the times, Christians who believe in biblical values and want to preserve them for the next generation, need to heed the warning of Professor Daniel Freedman, chairman of the Department of Psychiatry at the University of Chicago: "Society keeps testing things out. Is this the way we want it, or is that? . . . No matter how free we are we still make choices for ourselves. The adults deserve a lot of sympathy for living in this society, but if we don't begin to sort this out for them, God help the children."[12]

8
The Control Room at Home

An ancient philosopher posed a crucial question for parents when he asked, "And shall we just carelessly allow children to hear any casual tales which may be devised by casual persons, and to receive in their minds ideas for the most part the very opposite of those which we would wish them to have when they are grown up?"

Plato asked this question in *The Republic* more than 2,000 years ago. Yet it strikes right at the heart of the television issue today. Parents who carelessly ignore TV's influence are relinquishing control over much of their children's educational, value, behavioral, and personality development to the casual care of some far-distant and unknown television programmer.

For parents determined to protect their children and themselves from those "casual tales" and their deleterious ideas, the most logical, immediate

111

defense would be a home remedy. Yet, surprisingly little control is provided in the home.

Despite mounting publicity and the growing public awareness of television hazards, viewing time has continued to increase. In the average home, the set is turned on for the equivalent of almost two days a week. Many viewers not only neglect any sort of quantity control, they don't attempt to control content quality either. *Newsweek* reported that "a recent survey showed that a lethargically loyal 33 per cent of the video audience will stick with just one channel between 8 and 11 p.m.—no matter what is on."[1] In other words, millions of viewers won't even bother with the simple regulatory action of getting up and changing stations.

Even parents of young children, who should be most concerned, seem disinclined to regulate TV in their homes. In one study of children's viewing habits, only 16 percent of the mothers of first-graders restricted their children's viewing.[2]

After studying a number of other surveys, George Comstock, head researcher and editor of the Surgeon General's report on "Television and Social Behavior," concluded, "Television for young persons is an experience largely devoid of direct parental influence. Parents typically do not attempt to control quantity or character of viewing. Even in a sample of nursery-school children, 40 percent said they made their own program selection."[3]

The morning after the 1977 rerun of "Helter Skelter," one preschool teacher asked a table of ten middle-class four-year-olds how many of them had watched it the night before. Four of the ten raised their hands to indicate they had watched this movie version of the blood-curdling brutal and sordid Manson murders. And this was the rerun—after the well-publicized protests and public outcry that accompanied the first showing.

"My student teacher was shocked," reported the veteran preschool educator who conducted the informal survey. "But from my experience, I'd say the four-out-of-ten ratio was fairly representative."

Such a lack of parental sensitivity and control may be particularly alarming in the case of a program like "Helter Skelter," but its fits the general pattern. Various studies and audience surveys indicate children spend more time watching adult-type programming than they do viewing shows designed for children.

The president of American Broadcasting Companies, Inc., Elton H. Rule, talked about the role of parents in controlling children's television viewing in a speech he delivered to the Rotary Club of Los Angeles. He discussed a Roper Organization poll on parental rules in the home. The poll found that a sizable majority of parents had strict rules about what their children ate, when they went to bed, when they did homework, when they left the house, and where they were going.

But the poll also discovered that only two-fifths of the parents had rules about which programs their children could watch. And less than a third of the parents with children under twelve prohibited viewing after the family hour ended.

"What this appears to mean," concluded Rule, "is that parents who take active charge of most of the elements of their children's upbringing allow a kind of anarchy to prevail where television viewing is concerned."[4]

There are some encouraging exceptions. When parents have exhibited some degree of control, they've reported heartening signs. Fifteen Connecticut families that volunteered for a *Redbook* experiment found that a reduction in TV viewing time produced some amazing results. After the initial withdrawal symptoms had passed, parents and teachers noticed increased creativity, better socialization, improved family communication, and in at least one case, a drastic improvement in school work.[5]

A midwestern family noticed similar benefits after concern over TV's influence on their children prompted the parents to "turn off the set and see what happens." Three weeks into the experiment, the mother of five who ranged in age from four to fifteen beamed, "It's been great! I've never seen our kids have so much fun just playing games, talking, and doing things together."

Another family found themselves faced with involuntary control when their set malfunctioned, but enjoyed the change so much they didn't bother to have the set repaired for a year. During that time their fifth-grader had so much new free time that he read more than two hundred books.

Results like these have prompted a few parents to combat the effect of TV on their families by banning the tube completely. But despite the possible benefits of permanently pulling the plug, the practicality and wisdom of such a drastic measure is questionable. Prohibiting viewing does effectively eliminate any ill effects TV might have in the home, but any potential positive effect is missed as well.

There is another drawback to consider. A complete ban on TV in the home may just be avoiding or postponing the problems instead of dealing with them. Children from homes without TV can often visit friends to watch whatever they want. And some grow up, get married, and buy a set for their own homes without ever having a good example of how to use or control TV.

Perhaps a more beneficial remedy is one advocated by a couple with four school-aged children. The parents go through the *TV Guide* and mark "No!" in front of forbidden shows and "Yes!" opposite programs they approve of. If there is no "Yes!" for a particular time slot, the kids have to shut off the set and find other activities.

Another Christian family devised a strategy that allows the children to make their own decisions. At the beginning of the week, each child looks through the TV schedule and selects one hour of television he wants to watch. Occasionally, if the parents see that something else worthwhile is scheduled, they may invite the family to get together for the viewing. But usually the children are limited to one hour's worth of television of their choice.

Neither of these solutions would be perfect for every home. But all Christian parents should establish some standard of control to begin to battle the box and the inroads it is making into family life.

Any well-thought-out system of in-home control means parents have to find out which shows are worth watching. They will have to tune in with the kids. And for millions of mothers and father who don't even know what their children regularly see on the set, a critical viewing may be an eye-opening experience. Sometimes even parents who think they know can be in for a surprise.

Mrs. Nancy Sievert, chairman of the Christian Education Commission of the First Congregation Church of Vancouver, Washington, had suggested that her sons, ages seven and ten, watch the first episode of the "Ten Who Dared" series. It was to be about Christopher Columbus.

> I explained to my boys that it would be very educational and I thought they should watch it. Keep in mind that this program was shown between 7 and 8 p.m., the prime evening viewing hour for children. We settled ourselves in front of the TV set and it was not long before we saw a woman nude from the waist up, people being whipped by their captors, and a fairly explicit rape scene. Needless to say, I was appalled because there was no "parental discretion advised" warning either in the *TV Guide* or preceding the program to indicate that mature subject matter was to be shown.
>
> Instead of jumping up to turn off the TV—which I felt would be even more detrimental—I tried to answer my children's questions about why the men were whipping those poor people and about what they were doing to that lady. But the question that haunts me is: what if my children had seen that show by themselves? What kind of disturbing thoughts might have lingered in their minds if I had not been there to answer their questions?[6]

The Control Room at Home

This example illustrates the value of parental presence and supervision with the set. But Mrs. Sievert's experience also indicates that just knowing what children are watching and even watching with them may not be enough. For parents to effectively control and combat the harmful effects of TV on their children, they have to do what this mother did. They must be prepared to interact with their children about what they are seeing.

For example, a junior-high son of one Christian father wanted to watch one of the more explicit adult sit-coms. His father hesitated, then agreed—if they watched it together and if the boy promised to keep a tally of every suggestive or shady line he noticed.

Less than halfway into the show, the boy turned to his father and said, "I see what you mean. I've counted fourteen already. Why don't we turn to something else?" They came to a joint agreement not to watch the program anymore.

This kind of interaction takes sensitivity, concern, and a great deal of time and effort on the part of parents. But the effort brings rewards. A number of experiments demonstrate that adult interaction with children in front of the tube can make a significant difference in the effect of the televised action on young viewers. Many harmful effects can often be neutralized when adults help children interpret, discuss, and question TV content; even learning and positive effects of such shows as "Sesame Street" and "Mr. Roger's Neighborhood" are enhanced when adults reinforce what the children see on the screen.

Watching with children doesn't just give parents a barometer reading on what's fair and what's foul. For sensitive Christian parents, family viewing offers the bonus of invaluable time for interaction and guidance. Parents and children can share their feelings about the programs. They can discuss the values or lack of values a specific show promotes, and compare TV's standards with Christian principles. They can reach joint decisions on what should be watched, with the assurance that the reasons will be understood. When used wisely, TV can serve as a laboratory of life where a wide range of realistic situations outside the norm of Christian family experience can be observed and discussed to help young people learn and understand appropriate Christian responses and attitudes.

This doesn't mean that anything and everything on the set ought to be watched, assuming that "the kids will learn from the exposure." Discussion will not disarm every threat from the set. Some arbitrary parental decisions still have to be made about what and how much should be watched, especially for younger children. But a deliberate combination of control and careful utilization can help transform the family television from a threat to a positive force.

To do that, to become masters of the medium instead of its helpless victims, families need to establish and follow some system of control. Whether a family adopts some other family's method or devises an original plan of its own for curtailing television's impact, there are a number of general guidelines to keep in mind.

First, a family needs an accurate inventory of its

viewing habits. Parents can easily underestimate the amount of viewing their family engages in. Those who keep a close record for a week or a month may be surprised how the hours add up. That awareness alone may provide the incentive needed for additional control.

Second, a family needs to plan its viewing in advance. Many viewers switch the set on for the same reason some mountain climbers scale a peak: "Because it's there." Too many viewing decisions are made by default. The tube is turned on if there's nothing else to do. And then, if nothing particularly appealing is on, the channels get changed to the least objectionable program.

To make the most valuable use of TV, a family needs to base viewing decisions on something more than boredom or whims. Some sort of TV schedule is a necessity. The Television Information Office publishes a semi-yearly *Teacher's Guide to Television* for upcoming specials and programs of interest (see Appendix). But even *TV Guide* or the local newspaper's weekly TV listings can offer a look ahead as enticement for the good as well as a warning for the bad. The basis of deciding which is which and the limits on time may vary greatly with individual families. But without some kind of predetermination, there can be little effective home control.

The third step in a home defense against the influence of television on children and family life is to set proper priorities. As early as 1961, when television was relatively young, communications specialist Wilbur Schramm observed, "Overnight a new box appears in the home and thereafter all leisure is organized around it."[7] Too often this is true; television can easily become the major determinant of family schedules and activities. In order to control the influence of TV on its family, parents not only need to control the quantity and quality of viewing, but TV viewing itself must be prioritized.

One graduate student vividly remembers how his parents kept TV in perspective.

> One day when I was ten, my dad came home from the college where he taught. He told me a drama group wanted me to play the part of a young boy in a college production. Dad said the decision was up to me and explained what my participation would involve.
>
> I was thrilled until I heard the schedule of practices. The rehearsal time conflicted with "Zorro," my favorite TV show. So I immediately said no.
>
> But as soon as Dad heard my reasoning, he became very stern. I don't recall his exact words, but he said something like, 'We don't let television decide what we do or don't do.' Then he made a new rule. No television during rehearsal times whether I acted in the play or not. That made me mad, but I decided I may as well join the cast. As a result of that decision and of my dad's firm wisdom, I not only gained an invaluable experience in that drama, but I also learned the equally invaluable lesson that real life takes priority over any action on the tube.

That lesson, firmly taught and adequately learned, can transform the role of television in the home and in the lives of young viewers from dictator to servant.

The Control Room at Home

Fourth, a family needs to learn to see what it is watching. Too many people absorb and accept the sex, the violence, the unreality, and all the other TV content without any consideration of the consequences. They mainline the medium's message without filtering it through even the coarsest mental screen. Their viewing and their thinking seem totally separated. Yet a little critical attention could be one of the most effective insulations against the harmful effects of the electric eye.

This is where interaction comes in. It can teach viewers, both children and adults, to think for themselves—to become active viewers. While that may not control what comes out of the set, it can certainly alter what goes into the minds and lives of the people in front of the set. And that's the ultimate objective of control, anyway.

This chapter on the importance of controlling TV's impact in the home began with an old question from Plato. Parents ought to consider another old question—from Jesus: "What man is there of you, whom if his son ask bread, will he give him a stone? Or if he ask a fish, will he give him a serpent?"

Parents must face the evidence and recognize the potential threat TV presents to their families. For the welfare of their children and themselves, they must respond. The easiest place to begin is with the channel selector and the on-off switch. If parents don't take that responsibility, they are guilty of allowing their children to learn and grow and subsist on a source that is certainly no more nutritious than a stone and perhaps more dangerous than any serpent

9
Fighting Back: Fencing in the Dump!

Fortunately, the menace of television and its influence is beginning to dawn on the American public. As the awareness and the alarm grow, so do the ranks of outspoken opponents who are not content to stop with a strategy of home control.

More and more troubled viewers are adopting the attitude quoted by former Federal Communications Commissioner Nicholas Johnson: "I am qualified to criticize television because I have two eyes and a mind, which is one more eye and one more mind than television has."[1] These self-appointed critics are carefully examining themselves and their children for signs of video-fallout, and they're getting angry about what they find. They're demanding corrective action—not just in the home, but from within the broadcasting industry itself.

One of the earliest citizen's groups to take a militant stand in the battle on behalf of television's juvenile viewers was Action for Children's Television (ACT). This movement, which began in 1968 as the brainchild of four angry Massachusetts mothers, has spawned affiliate organizations in most states and now boasts more than 5,000 dues-paying members. This one group has probably done as much as any other single factor to keep the television issue exposed to the scrutiny of the press, the government, and the public. Through numerous articles written for the national media, through its own hearings and its testimony before government officials, and through its educational and protest activities, ACT has gathered widespread support for its cause.

The Parent-Teacher Association (PTA) is another group that has spoken strongly about television. At its 1975 national convention, the PTA adopted a resolution calling for concern and protest about televised violence. When the networks' reactions amounted to little more than a few corporate yawns, the PTA instituted a four-phase battle plan. The organization appointed a commission and thoroughly briefed the task force with expert training on every facet of the problem. That was phase one, in the fall of 1976.

Phase two consisted of a series of eight public hearings in major cities around the country during the winter of 1977. In those unprecedented proceedings, PTA members, public officials, broadcast spokesmen, and the public voiced their concerns and opinions about violence on the screen.

On April 5, 1977, the PTA stepped up its campaign by calling on members to keep a log of programs they watch and to launch a barrage of protest letters to stations and advertisers. Mrs. Carol Kimmel, the national president, also announced that as part of phase three of its campaign, the PTA was placing the networks on a six-month probationary period beginning July 1, 1977. She threatened that if the networks don't respond, phase four would include boycotts of advertisers, programs, and stations, and perhaps even legal action to deny license renewals.

The final effect of this action may not be fully realized for years. But the PTA endeavor is the most thorough, all-encompassing plan yet designed to attack the TV issue. With its organization, its numbers, and its strategy, the PTA's siege on the television industry is bound to cause consternation and gain some concessions from within the bastion of broadcasting. In fact, by the time the nationally publicized hearings concluded and the determined strength of the opposition was displayed, the networks had quit yawning and started talking about establishing diplomatic relations to discuss mutual concerns.

Another group in the forefront of the television battle has been the National Citizen's Committee for Broadcasting. The NCCB regularly monitors and criticizes the networks in its newsletter, *Media Watch*. In December, 1976, the committee stirred up a real ruckus among advertisers and the industry when it published a ranking of the networks, sixty-three shows, and 127 advertisers in order of violence.

In the wake of the protests and the public attention aroused by these groups, a number of Christian organizations and churches have established programs of their own to focus on television-related problems. The Southern Baptist's Christian Life Commission sponsored a series of public hearings in early 1977 to draw attention to the issues, to offer concerned criticism from a Christian perspective, and to gather testimony to present in protest to industry executives and officials of federal regulatory agencies.

The National Council of Churches' Communication Commission recently protested to those CBS affiliates that broadcasted the movie "Death Wish," which included vigilante violence. The United Methodist Church, the American Lutheran Church, and the Church of the Brethren have also applied pressure on the industry. And these three denominations, in conjunction with Media Action Research Center, recently launched a cooperative project called Television Awareness Training. This project has the goal of providing materials and trained leaders to conduct action and awareness workshops throughout the country.

So far, however, the majority of Christian response to the television issue has originated and remained at the official or denominational level. Despite the fact that Christians by nature should be more sensitive to and disturbed by television's sins, the grass-roots voice of the American Christian community—of local churches, of Christian parents, and of individual Christians—has been barely audible.

One grass-roots campaign that did gain national attention started when a United Methodist pastor from Southaven, Mississippi, called on his congregation to observe "Turn Off the Television Week." The minister informed the local press of his plan and when the story moved on the wire services, the national media took notice. Reverend Donald E. Wildmon received calls from more than two hundred newspapers and radio stations that wanted to know what was going on. An undetermined number of viewers joined in the protest. But before the week even began, Reverend Wildmon's postman delivered more than a thousand letters of support from well-wishers around the nation.[2]

The Church of God (Cleveland, Tennessee) mounted a similar viewing boycott on a denominational scale when it called on members of its congregation to turn off their sets for the entire week of April 11–18, 1977.

Four days after the ban ended, a spokesman for the church's Family Services Commission, which sponsored the action, admitted that an accurate gauge of participation was difficult. But he said officials estimated close to one million of the church's constituents took part in this first step of a denominational plan to focus attention on the trouble with TV. He explained that later steps would involve members in evaluating the impact of TV on their families, in rating shows, in letter-writing, and perhaps even in boycotts if networks and sponsors didn't respond satisfactorily by January, 1978.

No doubt these plug-pulling protest weeks aroused some awareness and provided a sense of I-did-something satisfaction for the non-viewers who participated. But unless a group had some sort of follow-up plans (such as the Church of God had), the impact of any viewing boycott was limited.

Perhaps if viewers across the country mounted a concerted movement for a "turn-off" protest, the networks would politely listen. But even then the industry could rest assured that the action wouldn't last long. For any turn-off tactic, whether for short-term protest or long-term solution, would be severely hampered by the national addiction to the television medium.

The futility of banning TV is graphically illustrated by the circumstance of one retired midwestern couple. Both were active attenders and participants at a very conservative church. They enjoyed and appreciated the fellowship and the spiritual atmosphere of their congregation. But the church had a long-established policy forbidding members to own television sets. Their solution to the dilemma was ingenious, if somewhat questionable. Only the wife joined the church. The husband could always attend with her. And both could continue to enjoy *his* television set in all good conscience.

It's that kind of attraction, an allurement that for some people can be even stronger than the attraction of spiritual fellowship and membership in a local church, which so discourages opponents who are trying to force change in the television industry. And it's the knowledge and assurance of this attractiveness that has made the networks so unresponsive to demands that they clean up their acts. They have ignored most criticism, offered occasional expressions of concern and claims of innocence, and continually defended the overall quality of their programming.

The best explanation for this lack of corporate conscience can be summed up in one word: money. Larry Gelbart, co-producer of *M.A.S.H.*, told *Newsweek* magazine, "I don't think that with the networks' obsession about profits they are going to change a system that's so good for them. They replace one bad show with another bad show and their profits grow every quarter. Even when they lose they win."[3]

Newsweek also quoted CBS programming chief Lee Currlin, who said, "Nothing short of an economic depression would prevent this industry from remaining profitable."[4]

But disgruntled viewers can take heart. There may be the artificial equivalent of a depression in the making. Reacting viewers are shifting their attacks from the networks to the industry's financial Achilles' heel—the advertisers. The NCCB ranking of companies by the amount of violence they sponsored caught a number of embarrassed advertisers blood-red handed. As a result of that adverse publicity and increased consumer pressure from other citizen action groups, many of TV's biggest advertisers hastily drew up anti-violence standards for sponsorship and allied themselves with the movement to reduce violence on TV. With additional pressures from the PTA and others, more advertisers will beat a retreat from violent series. And then, when the pinch comes from the pocketbook, industry officials will have to respond.

Other encouraging signs have emerged from various citizen action movements. ACT has perhaps been the biggest thorn in the side of television over the last decade. Progress has been slow, but measurable. In response to ACT and similar groups, the National Association of Broadcasters reduced the amount of advertising allowed on children's TV, a number of large drug companies withdrew their advertising from children's shows, and all three major networks appointed new vice-presidents for children's programming.

Even local action groups are wielding an influence. The Lansing (Michigan) Committee on Children's Television pressured local stations into originating some innovative shows for young viewers. Other groups around the country have spurred local stations to adopt higher programming standards and to become more responsive to the public's interest.

Even though network response has been limited, there is reason for optimism. Some progress has been made. Even more can occur if all Christian parents develop a stronger sense of moral conviction and social responsibility and get involved in the television issue. They might seriously consider taking a stand with the PTA or some other citizen group. They should at least encourage and support any action or awareness program sponsored by their denomination or other Christian group.

In considering a Christian-community response to television, believers might also take a cue from a number of other minority groups who have experienced some success in influencing TV content.

Homosexual activists, for instance, persuaded seventeen ABC affiliates not to air a "Marcus Welby" program about a psychopathic homosexual schoolteacher. They also prompted NBC to change a "Police Woman" episode that portrayed three lesbians as murderers.[5]

Women's groups have protested television's sex role stereotypes, and minorities as diverse as blacks, Puerto Ricans, and Poles have voiced their views to the industry, sometimes getting results. Norman Lear, the undisputed potentate of television sitcoms, now gives advance screenings of some of his shows to minorities. Their comments are then discussed by his writers in consciousness-raising sessions.

In light of what other minorities have accomplished, perhaps Christians could voice their own concerns. They might protest the absence of moral and spiritual values on so many shows. They could complain about the use of Bible-spouting religious fanatics as "villains" on so many shows, or even the way Christians are so often stereotyped on TV.

There may be some hope for redress if the Christian community would take such a special-interest-type approach. In a speech before an annual meeting of Christian broadcasters, Virginia Carter, vice-president of Norman Lear's TAT Communicatiions, acknowledged that television tends to deal in stereotypes, particularly of religious people, because "we are limited in what we know."

"We can only create shows out of our life experiences and what is in our heads," the programming official said. "If we talk to each other we can change the creation by changing what's in our heads."[6]

Ms. Carter went on to tell the gathering of Christian communicators that "remarkably few" viewers ever expressed themselves directly to the originators of the shows. She said that even twenty to fifty letters on a prime-time program would be considered a high number for a producer's mailbag.

With that in mind, any and every Christian parent who's aware of and concerned about television's influence on viewers—especially on children—ought to make his or her feelings and opinions known. Personal response could make a significant difference.

Even if the networks continue a stonewalling policy, local stations, television producers, and TV sponsors will listen. And since they're in a position to exert maximum pressure on the giant industry networks, a broad tidal wave of protest could be just the thing to inspire corrective action.

Individual viewers who decide to express their views should start with the local station. They can easily telephone the station to share an immediate opinion on any commendable or objectionable program or commercial. But even a call should be followed up with a letter. Local stations will read letters; they're required by FCC rules to keep on file all letters commenting on programming. Viewers should also send copies or separate letters to the network, the producer, and the sponsors responsible for the program being commented on. (Additional guidelines for letter-writing and a list of addresses are provided in the Appendix on page 153).

Fighting Back: Fencing in the Dump

Whatever response Christian viewers decide to take—whether it is involvement in one of the action groups, support of church programs aimed at the television problem, or just individual letter-writing, there's a hazard they need to be aware of. A lot of people, including some Christians, attack television as if it alone is responsible for all the violence and corruption in American society. We must realize that lambasting television as *the* scapegoat for society's sins is as ridiculous as pinning the blame for Adam and Eve's trouble in the Garden of Eden on the apple.

If the profusion of evidence proves anything, it is that television is an instrument contributing to a number of societal iniquities. As such, it deserves and demands Christian concern, criticism, and reaction. But the root problem remains the same as it has always been—the sinfulness of man. Christians need to keep that in perspective.

That doesn't mean Christians ought to open a hell-fire-and-damnation attack on the entire broadcasting industry. Little will be accomplished by being pushy or preachy. And Christians cannot realistically expect a secular industry in a secular society to closely conform to their set of scriptural standards.

But that doesn't preclude the possibility of a Christian response being recognized for its biblical basis. When believers oppose television's content and influence, they can and should make known the scriptural basis for their stand. If they can sensitively do so, their contribution to the easing of a serious social problem will be greatly appreciated by the public. And their involvement will serve as an unmistakable witness of Christian social concern.

A survey of the television situation reveals cause for optimism. But the hope lies not in government regulation, nor in some slim chance that the television industry will adequately solve the problems of its own volition, but in the outspoken concern of an informed public and a concerned Christian community that will respond to the challenge of former FCC chairman Richard E. Wiley: "If you are concerned . . . say so—say so in your communities, say so to your local broadcasters, say so to the advertisers, say so to Hollywood, and say so to your elected officials. Through your intelligent expression of concern, perhaps a new commitment *will* emerge—a new commitment on the part of the broadcasting industry to upgrade their efforts and to rid them of material which is deleterious to the moral and spiritual values which undergird our great nation."[7]

Reverend Jesse Jackson, head of Operation P.U.S.H., said "the issue is not censorship, but sense and sensitivity."[8] Concerned Christians have a chance and an obligation to contribute some of that sense and sensitivity. They can do it by getting actively involved with a citizen group, by speaking out as a caring body, and by taking an individual stand against the trouble on the tube. They have a choice. But if Christians expect to combat the effects of television on themselves, their families, and on society, they need to face and make that choice.

10
Creating Some Alternatives

Today's television presents a clear and present danger for millions of susceptible viewers. The evidence is convincing. TV's corrupt and corrupting content justifies drastic viewer reaction and protest. It should sufficiently alarm responsible Christian parents and inspire them to take precautionary action in their own homes to protect their children and themselves from any harmful impact of the medium. More Christians need to begin worrying and start asking, "What can we do to curb the ill effects of television?"

But home controls and outspoken protests are only preventive, basic defensive strategies for combatting the trouble on the tube. Any well-rounded response demands some positive, corrective measures as well. If Christians want a meaningful, long-range solution to the TV problem, they need to ask and answer a second question: "What can we offer children and adult viewers that will wield a positive impact?" The prevention of harm should be an important initial goal, but Christians developing a strategy for television should be searching for ways to use the medium as a positive force of their own.

Regrettably, the recent uproar over TV's harmful effects on viewers has often drowned out the equally significant and more hopeful findings that TV's impact can also mean a beneficial influence on viewers. Christians need to recognize and understand this potential.

Dr. Robert M. Liebert of the State University of New York, together with a number of other distinguished researchers, conducted a very impressive study of TV's positive potential. They selected two episodes of "Lassie" to show to a test group of children. One of the shows contained a positive message showing altruistic behavior while the other program was neutral. The youngsters were divided into three groups to view one of the two "Lassie" episodes or another pleasant but neutral program. Then the researchers created an opportunity for the children to choose between acting selfishly or in a positive altruistic manner comparable to the prosocial "Lassie" show.

> The effects of the prosocial example embedded in an entertainment context were striking indeed. A single exposure to the prosocial "Lassie" show produced an almost 100 percent increase in children's altruistic behavior. Thus, prosocial television examples foster prosocial behavior just as anti-social television examples foster anti-social behavior. The sig-

nificance of such a demonstration, we feel, can hardly be overstated. . . . The demonstration speaks to television's yet untapped benefits that could be realized in the future.[1]

The findings of a UCLA psychiatric department study on the effects of television viewing on the moods of adult watchers offer further encouraging proof of the tube's positive potential.

An experiment with 183 adult males, ages twenty to more than seventy, indicated TV can have both positive and negative influences on viewers. Participants who watched violent programs tended to be more personally aggressive and irritable. But those who viewed "helpful" or prosocial shows for a week were more even-tempered, attentive, and helpful toward their families—as judged by their wives and as measured by psychological testing. The experiment's results prompted the UCLA researchers to conclude, "We have evidence in this instance that helpful, prosocial television drama was capable of reducing ordinary hurtful behavior."[2]

But laboratory experiments don't provide the only indication that entertainment television can be a potential plus. Other positive effects have emerged from the experience of some innovative educators. In Chicago, Prime Time School Television has used the good and the bad content of network programming as the basis for students' classroom discussion. These discussions accomplish in a classroom setting what was suggested in Chapter 8 that parents do individually.

In 1970, educators in Philadelphia started what

they called a TV Reading Program where homework assignments were tied in with television programs. Thousands of scripts for the 1976 showing of the documentary drama "Eleanor and Franklin" were distributed before the broadcast. "An estimated 84 percent in the target group, grades 7 through 12, watched the show with their families while following along in the printed script."[3]

The Philadelphia program has obtained scripts for some of the regular series as well in an attempt to create greater interest in reading and to serve as the basis for class discussions on issues, content, and even writing techniques. Evidently the strategy works. Philadelphia school libraries "reported a 43 percent increase in borrowing that was directly attributable to the TV Reading Program."[4] Even though TV often gets blamed for being an enemy of reading and learning, it doesn't have to be. Television can, if wisely and creatively used, arouse interest and inspire viewers in their quest for knowledge.

Unfortunately, any prosocial effects of TV have been the exception in the overall impact of the medium. But that picture could change. The positive potential is there. The federal government's special violence commission concluded, "The producers of television programs have access to the imaginations and knowledge of the best talents of our times to display the full range of human behavior and to present prominently and regularly what is possible and laudable in the human spirit. They have time to think and experiment, and they have the entire history of man from which to draw."[5]

The hope hinted at by the violence commission's

report sometimes shines through on the screen. Public and commercial television sometimes offer fascinating documentaries, delightful comedies, and beautifully gripping human dramas that eloquently speak to the human spirit.

No one can watch a Jacques Cousteau program on marine life, or one of the "National Geographic" specials on some wonder of nature without being awed by the beauty and complexity of God's incredible creation. No one can view the unfolding drama of a life of pain and pride in something like "The Autobiography of Miss Jane Pittman" without gaining a broader perspective and a deeper sensitivity to the social concerns of black Americans. No one can sit through a true story like "Something for Joey" without being moved by the love between a Heisman Trophy-winning college football player and his little brother who is dying of leukemia.

There have been and there will continue to be many such outstanding programs—gems glistening amidst the cheap paste of typical television presentations. Such shows may not be inherently Christian, but the messages they present, the feelings they elicit from the viewer, are clearly in accord with biblical principles. Christians, collectively and individually, ought to recognize and applaud quality programming.

However, it often seems Christians demand too much of secular producers. Instead of commending the laudable aspects of the media, they doctrinally dissect and condemn anything that doesn't snugly fit their own theological perspective. The TV movie "Jesus of Nazareth" was a case in point.

TELEGARBAGE

In the weeks before this film was aired, a number of conservative Christians attacked it as blasphemy, charging that it denied Jesus' diety. Yet, while the film did gloss over some of Jesus' miracles and added some interpretation of its own, many Christians were thrilled at the overall tone of the movie. Far from the refutation of the gospel some of its critics had accused it of being, "Jesus of Nazareth" was a beautifully poignant portrayal of Christ's life on earth.

In fact, the film's message was so powerful that one young Kentucky woman called a local minister to tell him she had just seen the first half of "Jesus of Nazareth" and wanted to become a Christian. The minister, Rev. Eugene Guerra of the United Methodist Church in Paint Lick, Kentucky, prayed with her as she accepted Christ into her life.

The next day, this young student pastor shared what had happened and told a little about the movie to another woman who hadn't even seen it. She too indicated a desire to accept Christ.

The impact of the movie on these two lives so impressed Rev. Guerra that he traveled to the NBC affiliate in Lexington, Kentucky, to tell the station management of the response he had had and to ask if they would provide some time after the concluding Easter broadcast for a formal invitation to Christ. The station responded by allowing Methodist evangelist Ford Philpot to immediately follow the movie's conclusion with a short spot explaining how viewers could invite Jesus of Nazareth into their own lives.

As a result of one minister's conviction, a secularly

produced movie that a few Christians criticized as blasphemous became a channel through which thousands of Kentuckians were confronted with an opportunity to find Christ and make His Good News a part of their own personal lives.

But if television is to become a consistent spiritual force in American society, Christians can't just be content to applaud or even use what secular broadcasting supplies. If TV is to project an effective gospel voice, the Christian community is going to have to carve out its own role in the medium.

Some Christians have, of course, been using television as an evangelistic tool for years. Many churches and organizations regularly purchase air time to broadcast their Christian message. A growing number of Christian groups have purchased or founded their own stations to transmit Christian programming.

When most people think of the Christian message on TV, they usually picture a dynamic evangelist or preacher. The Billy Graham Evangelistic Association budgets millions of dollars a year to buy national prime time on nearly three hundred United States stations. Oral Roberts wraps his messages in a sort of multipurpose musical entertainment package. Ministers of many large churches broadcast their regular Sunday morning services. Others produce programs with a Christian talk-show format. Shows such as the "700 Club" and the "PTL Club" are telecast around the country.

Recent years have seen a variety of Christian approaches. Catholic and Protestant groups have developed some thought-provoking spots. Campus

Crusade for Christ utilized short testimonies in conjunction with its "Here's Life" campaigns. Southern Baptist churches in Texas designed a number of witnessing spots using big-name Christians as part of their "Living Proof" multi-media witness campaign. With a broader strategy, a Canadian group has produced an award-winning Christian children's program—"Circle Square"—that is broadcasted throughout Canada during "kid-vid" prime time on Saturday mornings.

Obviously, the Christian message has not been absent from the airwaves. However, it may not have realized its maximum potential in any of these Christian approaches. Despite extensive research that proves people learn from what they *see* on TV, Christians using the medium have persisted in their preference to *tell* their message instead of showing it. This is not to suggest that Christian efforts haven't produced far-reaching effects. God has reached thousands of people through the "telling" approach of evangelistic crusade broadcasts. And no doubt many more have been helped by other Christian programs.

But in contrast to the potential appeal of television drama, former FCC commissioner Nicholas Johnson wrote, "Talking heads make for poor television communication." He advised that "creative people first have to 'drop out' of the traditional modes of communicating thoughts and learn to swim through the new medium of television."[6]

What this means for Christian communicators is that for maximum appeal, audience, and effectiveness, the untapped potential of prime-time network television ought to be considered. Stacks of recent research prove that dramatic entertainment can be an extremely effective teacher of unChristian behavior and attitudes. Why couldn't it teach scriptural values? In the same way Christians drop their spiritual defenses to accept and enjoy unChristian and sometimes anti-Christian television fare, non-Christians who would never stay tuned in to an evangelistic appeal might readily watch and accept a Christian message couched in the dialogue and plot of a professionally done drama.

The recent made-for-TV movie "Hey, I'm Alive" would be a good example of an approach Christians could take. This film, starring Ed Asner of the "Mary Tyler Moore Show" and Sally Struthers from "All in the Family," portrayed the true story of two people who survived fifty-six days in the Yukon wilderness after their private plane crash-landed, and how the man's belief in the Bible brought the miracle that saved them.

Surely from somewhere in the annals of Christian history and the broad realm of modern-day Christian life, Christian communicators could find, write, and produce similar stories—powerful human dramas that not only entertain, but that plumb the depths of human emotion and spiritual experience. Christians should take it seriously; there is a market for quality Christian drama and entertainment programming. New time slots are always waiting to be filled. From September to May of 1975–76, the networks cancelled forty-two weekly series. But even if the networks didn't have a spot, a growing number of successful shows are syndicated independently; Christians might go that route. Several advertisers discontented with the shortage of available network ad time have been talking about creating a fourth network of their own. If that happens, there will be a brand new market needing a whole new set of programs—an ideal opportunity for Christians to break into prime time.

But the key to any hope Christians have of utilizing evening entertainment television for Christian programming is competition. Any Christian show would have to hold its own against other shows in its time slot, and Christian producers would have to contend with the ratings system just as everyone else.

That means any Christian prime-time venture can't be patently religious without falling victim to the Least Objectionable Program theory. Blatant religion or preachiness would be objectionable to many viewers, even on a dramatic show. They'd soon switch channels and the networks would can the series.

Unfortunately, many Christians have traditionally felt that for a show to be "Christian," each program had to present the complete message of salvation and conclude with an open invitation to accept Christ. Some even argue that anything less can only be a weak-kneed, watered-down, unacceptable cop-out. But if the researchers are right in saying that millions of viewers are influenced by what they see acted out on their television screens, then it is high time Christians did some serious thinking about prime-time TV production, even if it means playing by the networks' ratings rules. And if millions of searching people are indeed tuning in to TV entertainment to find solutions for the problems in their own lives, Christians shouldn't hesitate to share some biblical answers in the form of positive, realistic, television drama, even if the message has to be low-key. Concern that such an approach has to "compromise the gospel" is unwarranted. Many professional communicators now believe a sensitively subtle portrayal of Christian attitudes and values may have more lasting influence on viewers in terms of their acceptance and attitude toward Christianity than an outright appeal for conversion that would turn off millions of viewers who hadn't already turned off their sets. A well-done Christian drama series could easily serve a pre-evangelistic purpose by challenging viewers' preconceived prejudices against the gospel and by slowly building a positive, receptive attitude toward its Christian message.

At the very least, any positive program with an underlying Christian basis will serve as an oasis of morality in the wasteland of commercial television. Without such involvement, television will be continually barren of any Christian alternatives to offset the impact of the sex, the violence, the materialism, and the other secular propaganda that marks most prime-time television today.

The president of the J. Walter Thompson advertising agency told the 1976 American Advertising Federation Convention, "Television, as it exists today, is a new kind of fact. . . . From early childhood on, people form a major part of their impressions from it. . . . It gives children and adults a great many ideas about life and the world in which they live. At six hours a day it is one of their principal occupations—and their major source of impressions." If Christians continue to ignore the potential of television drama and entertainment as a crucial communication channel for the gospel, one of the impressions viewers may get from their set is that Christianity doesn't have anything to say to them.

The very absence of Christian principles in the make-believe life of the screen may discount or negate the messages coming from the pulpits and sanctuaries of American churches. Christians need to remember that many viewers see TV as the mirror image of reality. The punch of its picture validates the ticket of everyday life and experience. So if there is no portrayal of faith on the set, millions of viewers will never grasp the relevance of Christian experience for their own lives.

To put this in perspective, suppose for a minute that some future historians or archaeologists want to study twentieth-century American culture. Our most obvious and significant records would be on film and video-tape. But what picture of Christianity would future historians find amidst the celluloid artifacts of this generation's television communication records? What conclusions would they draw about the relevancy of our religion if they studied the tapes of televised series in an attempt to decipher the character and quality of American life in this age? At best, they might detect hints of the existence of some sort of anemic faith—but certainly nothing of importance or centrality in everyday living.

Tragically, that's just the conclusion millions of viewers are reaching today as they watch commercial television with its gaping religious void. Until Christians take a greater part in today's most popular and powerful art form, that conclusion will prevail.

This broadcasting art presents "an opportunity and challenge to develop and present programming which involves adventure, excitement, drama, mystery, jeopardy, conflict, emotion—all the basic elements of the classic art of storytelling and imagery—but to do so without the needless concomitant of violent and sexual excess."[7] If Christians don't accept this challenge and contribute the vital element of faith to this art form, a powerful opportunity for witness may be lost—not only for our TV-hooked society, but for generations to come.

Effective Christian involvement in prime-time television will be a costly undertaking. It will take creative writers, actors, and production people to originate the kind of top-quality programming that can withstand secular competition and still appeal to the deep spiritual needs of millions of viewers. But there are more and more young Christians dedicating themselves and their talents to the cause of Christian broadcasting. They're ready and willing to tackle the challenge. And they feel there's enough money in Christian coffers to make a good start.

What is really needed is an awareness of the potential, a conviction of the need, and a demand for involvement on the part of the Christian community. Before any meaningful effort can be launched to make television the potent, positive Christian influence it can be, believers have to make this a high priority.

They must recognize that the need and the opportunities are immeasurable. The medium of television is here to stay. In fact, the experts and the scientists predict more uses for TV and an even greater dependency on the medium in the future. If Christians get involved now while the industry is still young, they will be able to grow and expand as the industry itself gains influence and importance.

Edward R. Murrow, a pioneer in television broadcasting, summed up its potential when he told a 1958 meeting of radio and TV news directors in Chicago: "This instrument can teach, it can illuminate; yes, and it can even inspire. But it can do so only to the extent that humans are determined to use it to those ends. Otherwise it is merely wires and lights in a box. There is a great and perhaps decisive battle to be fought against ignorance, intolerance, and indifference. This weapon of television could be useful."[8]

Christians can't afford to go into battle without it.

11
A Final Word

The following TV-age paraphrase from a church newsletter is titled, "The 23rd Channel."

The TV is my shepherd. My spiritual growth shall want. It maketh me to sit down and do nothing for His name's sake, because it requireth all my spare time. It keepeth me from doing my duty as a Christian because it presenteth so many good shows that I must see.

It restoreth my knowledge of the things of the world and keepeth me from the study of God's Word. It leadeth me in the paths of failing to attend the evening church services and doing nothing for the Kingdom of God.

Yet, though I shall live to be a hundred, I shall keep viewing my TV as long as it will work, for it is my closest friend. Its sounds and its pictures they comfort me.

It presenteth entertainment before me and keepeth me from doing important things with my family. It fills my head with ideas which differ from those in the Word of God.

TELEGARBAGE

Surely no good thing will come of my life because of so many wasted hours, and I shall dwell in my remorse and regrets forever.[1]

At first reading this paraphrase may seem to stretch its point. But it may be more apropos than most people are willing to admit. Television has established itself as an electric religion in our modern technological society. Viewers religiously attend to it, certainly with more enthusiasm and frequency than they attend the forms of traditional religion.

TV has usurped many of the functions of religion. It provides explanations for the way things are; it interprets reality by offering its own world view. It establishes standards and values for attitudes and behavior.

Television even exhibits many characteristics of traditional religion. "Its celebrities are its priests, the networks its demoninations, the ratings its morality, TV sets and antennae its shrines, regular viewing its worship, and programs its ritual."[2]

The doctrines of this telecult—its sex, its violence, its unreality, its materialism—pose a sinister threat to Christian life and thought. But the real danger isn't from any one televised incident or program, or even from one particular series—no matter how sexually perverse, violently offensive, or ethically corrupt.

The biggest threat is that TV's all-showing eye is also omnipresent. It blares continuously into the lives and minds of its viewers. Hour after hour. Day after day. Year after year. It batters away at even the strongest defenses until viewers may soften and begin to tolerate, accept, and perhaps even adopt the messages it presents on the screen.

Walt Whitman posed the problem well when he wrote in *Leaves of Grass:*

> There was a child went forth every day,
> And the first object he look'd upon, that object he became,
> And that object became part of him for the day or a certain part of the day,
> Or for many years of stretching cycles of years.

That repetitive barrage of broadcasting is the biggest threat of television for viewers—adults as well as children. It can be ignored no longer.

Individual believers, parents, and the Christian community as a whole must face these issues, learn the facts, and take a firm, creative stand in dealing with the problems posed by television today.

Appendix

Guidelines to Writing Protest Letters

The pen is mightier than the sword and it can help effect some changes in TV programming too. Here are some suggestions for writing effective letters.

1. Don't rely on "form" letters. An individually written and signed letter will carry more weight.

2. Be specific. Give dates, times, stations, etc. Tell precisely what you object to and why. Avoid sweeping generalities.

3. Don't be preachy. Don't offer long theological arguments, but state your position clearly and concisely.

4. Keep it short and to the point. One-page letters are best.

5. It's usually better to write with a tone of well-thought-out concern than to whip off an angry letter expressing your outrage.

6. Send copies or separate letters to everyone involved—local stations, networks, sponsors, and producers. (See following pages for addresses.)

7. Express appreciation for good aspects of television.

8. Ask for a response.

Addresses

Networks

American Broadcasting Company (ABC)
1330 Avenue of the Americas
New York, NY 10019

Columbia Broadcasting System (CBS)
51 West 52nd Street
New York, NY 10019

National Broadcasting Company (NBC)
30 Rockefeller Plaza
New York, NY 10020

Public Broadcasting Service (PBS)
485 L'Enfant Plaza West—S.W.
Washington, D.C. 20024

Government

Federal Communications Commission
1919 M Street, N.W.
Washington, D.C. 20554

Subcommittee on Communications
Senate Commerce Committee
U.S. Senate
Washington, D.C. 20510

Local Stations
Listen for the call letters and consult your telephone
book for the phone numbers and addresses.

Appendix

Producers

Get the producer's name from the credits at the opening or the close of the show. Then address your letter to the producer, c/o that show, at the network which carried the program.

Advertisers

For local sponsors, check the phone book for telephone and address. To find the addresses of national sponsors, you could call local offices and ask for the headquarters address. You could also check with your local library. Ask if they have the *Directory of Advertising Products and Programs by TV Sponsors;* it lists all products by name and provides the address of the manufacturer. Or you could write for a directory at:

Television Product Cross-Reference Directory
Everglades Publishing Co.
Everglades, FL 53929

Organizations

Action for Children's Television
46 Austin St.
Newtonville, Massachusetts 02160

National Citizen's Committee for Broadcasting
1346 Connecticut Ave., N.W.
Washington, D.C. 20036

National PTA
700 N. Rush
Chicago, IL 60611

TELEGARBAGE

The National Association for Better Broadcasting
2315 Westwood Blvd.
Los Angeles, CA   90064

The American Council for Better Broadcasts
120 E. Wilson
Madison, WI   53703

Morality in Media
487 Park Ave.
New York, NY   10022

Publications

Teachers' Guides to Television ($4 per year)
Television Information Office
P.O. Box 564
Lenox Hill Station
New York, NY 10021

Morality in Media Newsletter
   (free to members)
487 Park Ave.
New York, NY   10022

Help for Television Viewers Packet ($1.00)
Southern Baptist Christian Life Commission
460 James Robertson Parkway
Nashville, TN 37219

Footnotes

Chapter 1

1. *Chicago Tribune*, Feb. 25, 1977.
2. Tony Schwartz, *The Responsive Chord* (New York: Anchor Press, 1974), pp. 14–16.
3. Leslie J. Chamberlin and Norman Chambers, "How Television is Changing Our Children," *The Clearing House*, Oct., 1976, p. 54.
4. George Gerbner, testifying before a special presidential commission on violence.
5. Harry J. Skornia, *Television and Society* (New York: McGraw-Hill, 1965), p. 176.
6. Evelyn Kaye, *Family Guide to Children's Television* (New York: Pantheon Press, 1974), p. 16.
7. "TV Violence: The Worst Offenders," *McCall's*, Mar., 1975, p. 51.
8. Harry F. Waters, "What TV Does to Kids," *Newsweek*, Feb. 21, 1977, p. 66.
9. Douglas Cater, "The Intellectual in Video Land," *Saturday Review*, May 31, 1975, p. 13.
10. Joseph T. Bayly, "High Price of TV," *Eternity*, Feb., 1970, p. 40.

Chapter 2

1. Russell T. Hitt, "Giant in the Parlor," *Moody Monthly*, Feb. 1954, p. 12.

2. Eugene H. Methvin, "What You Can Do About TV Violence," *Reader's Digest*, July, 1975, p. 186.

3. *New York Times*, Mar. 19, 1939.

4. Edward Carnell, *Television: Servant or Master?* (Grand Rapids, Mich.: Eerdmans Pub. Co., 1950), preface.

5. Nicholas Johnson, *How To Talk Back To Your Television Set* (Boston: Little, Brown and Co., 1970), p. 27.

6. Carnell, *Television: Servant or Master?*

7. Hitt, "Giant in the Parlor," p. 11.

8. *Ibid*, p.13.

9. *Ibid*, p. 11.

10. Robert T. Bower, *Television and the Public* (New York: Holt, Rhinehart and Winston, 1973).

11. *Ibid*.

12. M. Larson, "One-Eyed Giant," *Moody Monthly*, Oct., 1966, p. 26.

13. Joseph Bayly, "High Price of TV," *Eternity*, Feb., 1970, p. 40.

Chapter 3

1. Eugene H. Methvin, "What You Can Do About TV Violence," *Reader's Digest*, July, 1975, p. 185.

2. *New York Daily News*, Mar. 12, 1974.

3. Victor B. Cline, "TV Violence: How It Damages Your Children," *Ladies' Home Journal*, Feb., 1975, p. 75.

4. Cited from Victor B. Cline, ed., *Where Do You Draw the Line?* (Provo, Utah: Brigham Young Univ. Press, 1974), p. 158.

5. Alberta Siegel, "Communication with the Next Generation," *Journal of Communications*, Autumn, 1975, p. 23.

6. Cline, *Where Do You Draw the Line?* p. 118.

7. *New York Times*, Dec. 21, 1966.

8. Grant H. Hendrick, "When Television is a School for Criminals," *TV Guide*, Jan. 29, 1977, p. 5.

Footnotes

9. *Ibid.*, p. 8.

10. Cline, *Where Do You Draw the Line?* p. 119.

11. *Ibid.*, pp. 119–120.

12. Albert Bandura, *Aggression: A Social Learning Analysis* (Englewood Cliffs, N.J.: Prentice-Hall, Inc., 1973).

13. *The Oregonian*, Jan. 20, 1977.

14. S. Clinton, "TV As a Behavioral Model: Results of Research," *American Education*, July, 1975, p. 40.

15. Ronald Drabman and Margaret Hanratty Thomas, "Does TV Violence Breed Indifference?" *Journal of Communications*, Autumn, 1975, p. 88.

16. Rex C. Ramsey, testifying before the PTA's public hearing in Dallas, Texas, on Feb. 1, 1977.

17. *Chicago Tribune*, Oct. 30, 1976.

18. Walter Menninger, testifying before the PTA's public hearing in Kansas City, Jan. 11, 1977.

19. Commission's report, "To Establish Justice, To Insure Domestic Tranqulity," 1969, p. 206.

20. Alberta Siegel, in her summary of the Surgeon General's report for the Subcommittee on Communications of the U.S. Senate Committee on Commerce, March, 1972.

21. Cline, *Where Do You Draw the Line?* p. 178.

Chapter 4

1. *Chicago Tribune*, Oct. 7, 1976.

2. *Ibid.*

3. Harry F. Waters, "The Mary Hartman Craze," *Newsweek*, May 3, 1976, p. 54.

4. *New York Times*, Nov. 21, 1976.

5. *Ibid.*

6. Ann Kaye, testifying before the PTA hearing in Hartford, Conn., Feb. 15, 1977.

7. Bertram S. Brown, testifying before the U.S. Senate Subcommittee on Communications, April, 1974.

8. Albert Bandura and Richard Walters, *Social Learning and Personality Development* (New York: Holt, Rhinehart and Winston, 1963), pp. 65, 76–78.

9. Harry J. Skornia, *Television and Society* (New York: McGraw-Hill, 1965), p. 155.

Chapter 5

1. Douglas Cater, "The Intellectual in Video Land," *Saturday Review*, May 31, 1975, p. 13.

2. *Advertising Age*, Jan. 17, 1977, p. 2.

3. "Price Is No Object in TV's New Season," *Business Week*, Sept. 6, 1976, pp. 22–23.

4. Harry W. McMahan, "Star Presenter Isn't Always Enough to Make an Ad Shine," *Adverstising Age*, Mar. 28, 1977, p. 62.

5. *Ibid.*

6. Harry W. McMahan, "Blast Your Company Name, Front and Center, Out of Ad Clutter," *Advertising Age*, Feb. 28, 1977, p. 56.

7. Mark Shedd, testifying before the regional PTA hearing in Hartford, Conn., Feb. 15, 1977.

8. Michael B. Rothenberg, "Effect of Television Violence on Children and Youth," *Journal of the American Medical Association*, Dec. 8, 1975, p. 1043.

9. Harry F. Waters, "What TV Does to Kids," *Newsweek*, Feb. 21, 1977, pp. 66, 69.

10. Thomas Bever and Martin Smith, "Young Viewers' Troubling Response to TV Ads," *Harvard Business Review*, Nov., 1975, pp. 109–120.

11. *Ibid.*, p. 119.

12. Neil Hickey, "It's Goodbye Brand X," *TV Guide*, Oct. 2, 1976, p. 46.

13. Tony Schwartz, *The Responsive Chord* (New York: Anchor Press, 1974), p. 73.

Footnotes

14. Robert Chew, "Three-Second Spots? Too Slow for 1992," *Advertising Age*, Mar. 21, 1977, p. 1.

15. Vance Packard, *The Hidden Persuaders* (New York: David McKay Co., Inc., 1957).

16. Roy Truby, testifying before a PTA hearing in Portland, Ore., Feb. 8, 1977.

17. D.G. Kehl, "The Devil's Electric Carrot," *Christianity Today*, Feb. 16, 1973, p. 20.

Chapter 6

1. Edward J. Carnell, *Television: Servant or Master?* (Grand Rapids, Mich.: Eerdman's Pub. Co., 1950), p. 168.

2. *New York Times*, Aug. 25, 1966.

3. George Gerbner and Larry Gross, "Living With Television: The Violence Profile," *Journal of Communications*, Spring, 1976, pp. 178–179.

4. *Philadelphia Bulletin*, July 10, 1974.

5. Douglas Cater, "The Intellectual in Video Land," *Saturday Review*, May 31, 1975, p. 14.

6. George Gerbner and Larry Gross, "The Scary World of TV's Heavy Viewers," *Psychology Today*, April, 1976, p. 41.

7. Cited from Victor B. Cline, ed., *Where Do You Draw the Line?* (Provo, Utah: Brigham Young Univ. Press, 1974), p. 216.

8. Bruce Baker, testifying before a PTA hearing in Portland, Ore., Feb. 8, 1977.

9. Marshall McLuhan, *Understanding Media: An Extension of Man* (New York: McGraw-Hill, 1974), p. 292.

10. Gerbner and Gross, "Living With Television," p. 176.

11. Joe Bayly, "High Price of TV," *Eternity*, Feb., 1970, p. 41.

12. Gerbner and Gross, p 182.

Chapter 7

1. Harry F. Waters, "What TV Does to Kids," *Newsweek*, Feb. 21, 1977, p. 65.

2. Jeffrey Schrank, "There Is Only One Mass Medium: A Resource Guide to Commercial Television," *Media and Methods*, Feb., 1974, p. 32.

3. Timothy P. Meyer, "Impact of 'All In the Family' on Children," *Journal of Broadcasting*, Winter, 1976, p. 23.

4. Claire Safran, "How TV Changes Children," *Redbook*, Nov., 1976, pp. 88–97.

5. Schrank, "Guide to Commercial Television," p. 331

6. Waters, "What TV Does to Kids," p. 65.

7. *Chicago Tribune*, Mar. 30, 1976.

8. Doyle Aultman, testifying before a PTA hearing in Kansas City, Jan. 11, 1977.

9. "Hidden TV Messages Create Social Discontent," *Intellect*, Feb., 1976, p. 350.

10. Cecilia v Feilitzen and Olga Linné, "Identifying With Television Characters," *Journal of Communications*, Autumn, 1975, p. 54.

11. Marshall McLuhan, *The Medium is the Massage* (New York: Bantan Books, Inc., 1967), p. 14.

12. "What's Happening to American Morality?" *U.S. News and World Report*, Oct. 13, 1975, p. 41.

Chapter 8

1. Harry F. Waters, "Why Is TV So Bad?" *Newsweek*, Feb. 16, 1976, p. 73.

2. R. Liebert and R. Baron, "Television As Babysitter," *Child Development*, vol. 45, 1974, pp. 1132–1136.

3. George Comstock, "The Evidence So Far," *Journal of Communications*, Autumn, 1975, p. 27.

4. Elton H. Rule, "Children's Television Viewing," *Vital Speeches*, Oct. 15, 1976, p. 25.

Footnotes

5. Claire Safran, "How TV Changes Children," *Redbook*, Nov., 1976, pp. 88–97.
6. Nancy Sievert, testifying before a PTA hearing in Portland, Ore., Feb. 8, 1977.
7. Wilbur Schramm, *Television in the Lives of Our Children* (Stanford: Stanford Univ. Press, 1961), p. 169.

Chapter 9

Nicholas Johnson, "What Do We Do About Television?" *Saturday Review*, July 11, 1970, p. 15.
2. *Tampa Times*, Feb. 26, 1977.
3. Harry F. Waters, "Why Is TV So Bad?" *Newsweek*, Feb. 16, 1976, p. 74.
4. Harry F. Waters, "The Big 3's Big 3," *Newsweek*, Feb. 16, 1976, p. 75.
5. Harry F. Waters, "TV: Do Minorities Rule?" *Newsweek*, June 2, 1975, p. 78.
6. *Christian Citizen*, Feb., 1977.
7. Richard E. Wiley, "Violence, the Media, and the School," *NASSP Bulletin*, May, 1976, p. 24.
8. Rev. Jesse Jackson, testifying at the PTA hearing in Chicago, Jan. 25, 1977.

Chapter 10

1. Robert M. Liebert, sharing the results of the "Lassie" experiment in testimony before the U.S. Senate's Subcommittee on Communications, April 5, 1974.
2. Roderic Gorney, David Loye, and Gary Steele, "Impact of Dramatized Television Entertainment on Adult Males," *American Journal of Psychiatry*, Feb., 1977, p. 173.
3. Max Gunther, "How Television Helps Johnny Read," *TV Guide*, Sept. 4, 1976, p. 7.
4. *Ibid.*, pp. 7–8.

5. Commission's report, "To Establish Justice, To Insure Domestic Tranquility," 1969, p. 206.

6. Nicholas Johnson, "What Do We Do About Television?" *Saturday Review*, July 11, 1970, p. 15.

7. Richard E. Wiley, "Violence, the Media, and the School," *NASSP Bulletin*, May, 1976, p. 24.

8. Edward R. Murrow, "A Broadcaster Talks to His Colleagues," *The Reporter*, Nov. 13, 1958, p. 36.

Chapter 11

1. *Kentucky United Methodist*, Mar. 18, 1977.

2. Jeffrey Schrank, "There Is Only One Mass Medium: A Resource Guide to Commercial Television," *Media and Methods*, Feb., 1974, p. 33.